Commentary on UCP 600

Article-by-Article Analysis by the UCP 600 Drafting Group

ICC
International Chamber of Commerce
The world business organization

ICC Services
Publications Department
38 Cours Albert 1er
75008 Paris
France

ICC Publication No. 680
ISBN: 978-92-842-0015-3

Table of Contents

Introduction

During the revision of UCP 500, the UCP 600 Drafting Group provided regular feedback at ICC Banking Commission meetings concerning the issues currently under discussion. The feedback included areas of contention that had arisen from the comments received from ICC national committees, as well as the Drafting Group's thinking behind new concepts that were being incorporated into the text.

The contentious issues remaining to be decided led ICC to convene an extra meeting of the Banking Commission in Dublin in June 2005. This was particularly important, because with around 5000 comments received during the revision process, it was impossible for the Drafting Group to provide feedback on every issue that did or did not make it into the text of UCP 600.

These issues included, amongst others, the following items:

- Should the words "on its face" remain within the UCP?
- What was the value of the concept of "reasonable time" when there was no common standard for determining reasonableness globally?
- Should the UCP now reflect the growing practice of documentary credits being issued by non-banks, by substituting "issuer", "confirmer", etc., for the terms "issuing bank", "confirming bank", etc., that had been used in past UCPs?
- Was a majority of the Banking Commission in favour of including a rule covering the ability of a nominated bank to prepay or purchase a draft it accepted or a deferred payment it incurred?
- Was there a need for an equivalent of UCP 500 article 30 when the UCP transport document articles do not mention who is actually to "issue" the respective transport document?

All of the points were debated at some length by national committees tasked with providing input, so that the Drafting Group could gauge where their representatives on the Banking Commission wished an article to be positioned.

All of this is now history. The UCP 600 was unanimously approved by the Banking Commission in October 2006 and came into effect on 1 July 2007. But in keeping with other revisions of the UCP, the work of the Drafting Group did not cease with the approval of the rules or their implementation. Other UCP revisions have been followed by ICC publications comparing past versions of the rules with the new.

As experienced documentary credit practitioners know, UCP 600, whilst not containing many substantial changes in practice, does have a new style and structure. The introduction of new articles covering definitions and interpretations has brought together rules that existed in various sections of UCP 500. As examples, article 6 has combined wording from articles 9, 10 and 42 of UCP 500, whilst article 14 has wording from articles, 13, 14, 21, 22, 30, 31, 37 and 43 of UCP 500. With this in mind, the Drafting Group decided that a publication comparing one set of rules with another would be too unwieldy and that a Commentary on the rules themselves would prove to be more beneficial. The aim has been to provide a Commentary that enlightens practitioners to a number of the thought processes behind the changes in each article and to explain why a change was introduced, why no change was made, why some issues may appear new but are not, i.e., a clarification rather than a change, and to suggest the way the wording in UCP 600 should be understood and applied.

It is fair to say that writing this Commentary proved to be more difficult than drafting the rules themselves.

The Drafting Group must point out that the text of this Commentary reflects the views of the Drafting Group and not necessarily those of the ICC Banking Commission. Because the content contains information relating to the Drafting Group discussions and because there was a need for this publication to be in circulation as soon as possible after the implementation date of UCP 600, it was not passed through the Banking Commission for their approval.

Users of the Commentary should also be reminded that any decision to accept or reject documents should be based on the text of the underlying documentary credit and the applicable rules of UCP 600 and not the Commentary. As an accompaniment to the UCP 600, the ICC publication *International Standard Banking Practice for the Examination of Documents under Documentary Credits* (ISBP) has been updated (ICC Publication No. 681) for use with UCP 600. The ISBP, together with Opinions of the Banking Commission that will be approved and published from time to time, will additionally serve as valuable tools for parties to correctly apply the principles of UCP 600 and accurately interpret and clarify conditions appearing within documentary credits.

On behalf of the Drafting Group, I hope this publication will serve as a useful aid in your day-to-day transactions and will provide valuable insights into the thinking of the Drafting Group during the 3 ½ years of the revision process.

Gary Collyer

Technical Adviser, ICC Banking Commission

Chair, UCP 600 Drafting Group

ARTICLE 1

Application of UCP

The *Uniform Customs and Practice for Documentary Credits, 2007 Revision*, ICC Publication No. 600 ("UCP") are rules that apply to any documentary credit ("credit") (including, to the extent to which they may be applicable, any standby letter of credit) when the text of the credit expressly indicates that it is subject to these rules. They are binding on all parties thereto unless expressly modified or excluded by the credit.

CHANGES FROM UCP 500

- Style change in not capitalizing the term "credit";
- Reference to 2007 revision;
- Change in publication number;
- Introduction of the term "rules";
- Change to apply to "any" documentary credit rather than "all" in UCP 500;
- Change from "where incorporated in the rules" to "when the text of the credit expressly indicates that it is subject to these rules";
- Change to "unless expressly modified or excluded by the credit".

COMMENTARY

Article 1 introduces several changes to the UCP in style and substance related to the applicability of the rules.

The article introduces the term "rules" to refer to the UCP. Previous versions of the article have simply referred to the UCP. Whilst over the years the UCP have been referred to by practitioners as rules, the UCP itself has not previously used this term.

The article also changes the premise that the UCP are effective when they are incorporated into the text of the documentary credit, to the concept that they are effective when the text of the documentary credit expressly indicates that it is subject to the UCP. A number of questions were raised concerning the previous language when SWIFT was used to transmit the documentary credit. Unfortunately, despite clarifications in the SWIFT rules, the questions continued to be posed. Early in the drafting process, the Drafting Group decided to change the article to require express incorporation and asked SWIFT to make changes to its system to accommodate this change. These changes have been implemented by SWIFT within the SWIFT MT 700, 710 and 720 message standards so that the issuing bank is able to specifically indicate the applicability of the rules in the SWIFT message and the documentary credit.

Whilst the UCP now requires an express indication that a documentary credit is subject to the rules, where this express indication is not made and an indication of other rules is not present, the rules may be applied as descriptions of custom applicable to documentary credits.

In many cases in past versions of the UCP, the phrase "unless otherwise stipulated in the credit" or similar phrases were used in the articles. The Drafting Group decided that significant improvements in the style and readability of the rules could be made by eliminating this phrase throughout the rules. In order to make this change, it was decided that article 1 should state that a modification or exclusion should be expressly stated in the documentary credit itself. This inclusion in article 1 means that any article of the rules may be modified or excluded by express wording to that effect or by exclusion in the documentary credit.

During the course of the revision, a number of ICC national committees suggested that the reference to standby letters of credit be deleted from the UCP. Their rationale was that with the introduction of ISP98, there were now specific rules for standby credits. After considerable discussion, the Drafting Group felt that the reference to standby credits could not be deleted since, despite the introduction of ISP98, there were still a significant number of standby credits that continued to be issued subject to the UCP. The Drafting Group also believed that even if the reference were deleted, banks would continue to issue standby credits subject to the UCP.

In article 1, changes in style have been made to reflect the change in capitalization, i.e., the term "credit" is no longer capitalized, nor are other terms that have been capitalized in past versions of the UCP. Changes also include the inclusion of the publication number and the year of the revision.

Cross-references within UCP 600

- Definition of "Credit" contained in article 2.

Article 2

Definitions

For the purpose of these rules:

Advising bank means the bank that advises the credit at the request of the issuing bank.

Applicant means the party on whose request the credit is issued.

Banking day means a day on which a bank is regularly open at the place at which an act subject to these rules is to be performed.

Beneficiary means the party in whose favour a credit is issued.

Complying presentation means a presentation that is in accordance with the terms and conditions of the credit, the applicable provisions of these rules and international standard banking practice.

Confirmation means a definite undertaking of the confirming bank, in addition to that of the issuing bank, to honour or negotiate a complying presentation.

Confirming bank means the bank that adds its confirmation to a credit upon the issuing bank's authorization or request.

Credit means any arrangement, however named or described, that is irrevocable and thereby constitutes a definite undertaking of the issuing bank to honour a complying presentation.

Honour means:

a. to pay at sight if the credit is available by sight payment.

b. to incur a deferred payment undertaking and pay at maturity if the credit is available by deferred payment.

c. to accept a bill of exchange ("draft") drawn by the beneficiary and pay at maturity if the credit is available by acceptance.

Issuing bank means the bank that issues a credit at the request of an applicant or on its own behalf.

Negotiation means the purchase by the nominated bank of drafts (drawn on a bank other than the nominated bank) and/or documents under a complying presentation, by advancing or agreeing to advance funds to the beneficiary on or before the banking day on which reimbursement is due to the nominated bank.

Nominated bank means the bank with which the credit is available or any bank in the case of a credit available with any bank.

Presentation means either the delivery of documents under a credit to the issuing bank or nominated bank or the documents so delivered.

Presenter means a beneficiary, bank or other party that makes a presentation.

Changes from UCP 500

- New article to reflect the definitions of terms used in the UCP.

Commentary

Early in the process of the revision, the Drafting Group decided that as part of the process of simplification of the rules it would be desirable to create one article that contained the definitions of the principal terms used in the UCP. Article 2 is this article, and it includes all of the significant terms utilized in UCP 600. The exception to this is the terms applicable to transferable credits. The Drafting Group decided that because of their uniqueness, the terms specific to transferable credits were better contained in the article on transfer. As a result, those terms are contained in article 38.

In addition to the transferable credit terms, there are further definitions contained in article 9 (second advising bank), article 11 (pre-advice), article 13 (claiming bank and reimbursing bank) and article 37 (charges). These definitions were retained in the specific articles due to their unique relationship with the article.

The definitions of many of these terms are not new to the UCP, have been taken from the definitions that existed in UCP 500 and do not materially differ from the definitions found there. Most have been restructured or clarified so that they are complete when standing alone and are not part of an article. A number of the definitions are new and were added to aid in the simplification of the articles as a whole. For easy reference, each of the terms is listed below with a commentary.

Advising bank

The definition of advising bank was found in UCP 500 in sub-article 7 (a) and was simply defined by its usage – "A Credit may be advised to a Beneficiary through another bank (the 'Advising Bank')". The definition contained in UCP 600 simply states that it is the bank that advises the credit at the request of the issuing bank.

Applicant

UCP 500 defined the applicant of the documentary credit in article 2 in terms of the bank's customer. The UCP 600 definition defines the applicant as the party on whose request the documentary credit is issued. This definition has been broadened slightly to include a party on whose request the documentary credit is issued. This is to provide for the fact that the applicant can be someone other than strictly the "customer" of the bank. In today's practice, the applicant is often the customer of a correspondent bank or a subsidiary of the bank's customer. The use of the term "party" in the definition is not intended to include the applicant as a party to the documentary credit, but to reflect the concept that the applicant can mean an entity other than the bank's actual customer.

Banking day

The definition of "Banking day" includes two distinct principles: first, it includes the days on which the bank is regularly open, which, depending on the country, will not necessarily be the same days that are considered to be a weekend or a bank public holiday; second, the bank must be open to perform an act subject to the UCP. In other words, the bank must be open to handle one or more of the following processes: to issue, advise, amend, accept a presentation, examine a presentation or honour or negotiate a documentary credit. These two distinct principles help to better define the functions carried out under UCP 600 and to avoid the situation, for example, in which the bank may be open for retail business on a Saturday, but not open on that day to conduct documentary credit business.

Beneficiary

UCP 600 defines the beneficiary as the party in whose favour a documentary credit is issued.

Complying presentation

In order to simplify the text of UCP 600, the Drafting Group decided to define a complying presentation under a documentary credit. UCP 500 defined, in broad terms, a presentation that complied with a documentary credit in sub-article 13 (a) as "Compliance of the stipulated documents on their face with the terms and conditions of the Credit shall be determined by international standard banking practice as reflected in these Articles."

The UCP 600 definition of "Complying presentation" means a presentation that is in accordance with the terms and conditions of the documentary credit, the applicable provisions of these rules and international standard banking practice.

This definition includes three concepts. First, the presentation of documents must comply with the terms and conditions of the documentary credit. Second, the presentation of documents must comply with the rules contained in UCP 600 that are applicable to the transaction, i.e., those that have not been modified or excluded by the terms and conditions of the documentary credit. Third, the presentation of documents must comply with international standard banking practice. The first two conditions are determined by looking at the specific terms and conditions of the documentary credit and the rules themselves. The third, international standard banking practice, reflects the fact that the documentary credit and the rules only articulate some of the processes that banks undertake in the examination of documents and in the determination of compliance. International standard banking practice includes practices that banks regularly undertake in determining the compliance of documents. Many of these practices are contained in the ICC's publication *International Standard Banking Practice for the examination of Documents under Documentary Credits* ("ISBP") (ICC Publication No. 681); however, the practices are broader than what is stated in this publication. Whilst the ISBP publication includes many banking practices, there are others that are also commonly used in documentary credit transactions beyond those related to the examination of documents. For this reason, the definition of complying presentation does not specifically refer to the *International Standard Banking Practice* publication.

Confirmation

UCP 500 contained the definition of the undertaking of a confirming bank in sub-article 9 (b). The definition used in UCP 600 states the same principles while tying the definition to the UCP 600 defined terms for "Complying presentation", "Honour" and "Negotiation".

Confirming bank

A confirming bank in UCP 600 is simply defined as the bank that adds its confirmation to a documentary credit upon the issuing bank's authorization or request. UCP 500 defined the confirming bank in sub-article 9 (b).

Credit

Article 2 of UCP 500 contained the definition of a documentary credit in terms of the obligation and the basic parties to the documentary credit (issuing bank and beneficiary). UCP 600 combines the two parts of this definition and states that a documentary credit is any arrangement, however named or described, that is irrevocable and thereby constitutes a definite undertaking of the issuing bank to honour a complying presentation. The UCP 600 definition includes the general principle that all documentary credits under the rules are considered to be irrevocable; the concept of revocable documentary credits has been removed from UCP 600. The definition links the undertaking to the definitions of "Honour" and "Complying presentation".

Honour

UCP 500 defined the undertaking under a documentary credit by stating the three methods of fulfilling that undertaking – paying at sight, paying a deferred payment undertaking at maturity and accepting a draft and paying it at maturity. UCP 600 has used a drafting technique to employ a single term, "honour", for these three types of availability in order not to repeat them each time they appear in the rules. This technique allows the use of the term "honour" to simplify the text. A documentary credit, when issued, will state the method of availability, which is one of the three options, or use a combination of the options (termed "mixed payment") included in the term "honour" or by indicating that the documentary credit is available by negotiation.

Issuing bank

UCP 500 defined the issuing bank in article 2 simply as the bank that issued the documentary credit. UCP 600 defines "Issuing bank" in similar terms, meaning the bank that issues the documentary credit, linking the issuance to a request of an applicant or to a situation in which the documentary credit is issued by the issuing bank on its own behalf.

During the revision process, the issue arose as to the handling of documentary credits issued by non-banks. In October 2002, the ICC published its Opinion R. 505 (which is also available on the ICC website – www.iccwbo.org) with regard to the status of such documentary credits. This Opinion, which is reproduced below as TA 537, has equal standing under UCP 600.

QUERY **[TA 537]**

We have been receiving a significant number of enquiries about letters of credit which are advised by some banks in the usual way, but are actually issued by a corporate or the finance arm of the corporate and not a bank.

These predominantly corporate L/Cs from Country U are 'advised' by banks on their letterhead in a SWIFT MT 700 format, and to all intents and purposes appear to be bank-issued L/Cs, with the requirement to present documents to the advising or transferring bank, where documents will be processed and payment made after receipt of funds from the 'issuer'.

Invariably they incorporate clauses to the effect that the L/C is subject to the UCP, and that where the UCP refers to 'issuing bank' then the issuer is to be construed as acting in all respects as the 'issuing bank'.

Notwithstanding the fact that legally any entity can issue a letter of credit, our understanding is that the UCP only contemplates as issuers banks, on the basis that the issuing bank is undertaking a third party, independent guarantee of payment to the seller (beneficiary). It is this independence of a banker's letter of credit that is key to the payment undertaking.

The requirement by the seller for a letter of credit is two-fold: first, that he has a guarantee of payment, and second, that he can use the credit to raise pre-shipment finance from his banker.

In the case of the corporate L/C, as we understand it, the guarantee of payment is not normally by an independent third party, and, as such, the credit risk is that of the corporate entity issuing the credit. Similarly, when documents are presented under the L/C for negotiation, that negotiation, if any, is based on the risk of the issuing entity, i.e., is corporate, not bank risk.

We would be grateful if the ICC Commission on Banking Technique and Practice would advise on the following:

1. Is it acceptable practice for a bank to advise a corporate letter of credit in the same way as a bank-issued letter of credit without drawing attention to the 'non-bank' nature of the issuing entity? Does the Commission consider appropriate guidelines should be published? If so, what will these say?

2. What is the position if the corporate issuer were to apply for liquidation, bankruptcy, or protection from creditors (e.g., file for Chapter 11), and how different is the position to that of when a bank is unable to meet its obligations?

Analysis

The UCP reflects that state of practice, namely a situation where the issuer or other actor on a letter of credit is a bank. As a result, although there is no affirmative rule in the UCP prohibiting entities that are not banks from issuing, confirming, paying, negotiating, or advising letters of credit, its vocabulary ('issuing bank', 'confirming bank', etc.) assumes that these entities are banks.

This assumption is based on the recognition that there are three principal advantages to bank issuance and handling of letters: namely, that banks have the operational expertise to handle issuance and presentation under letters of credit in a professional manner, that they have the tradition of independence from the underlying transaction, which is the basis of the commercial reputation of the letter of credit, and that in virtually all countries banks are specially regulated with a view toward protecting those who rely on their undertakings.

These matters are of considerable importance to the integrity of the letter of credit as an instrument of commerce and to its dependability as an instrument of payment.

However, neither the Commission on Banking Technique and Practice nor the UCP can determine who is empowered to issue letters of credit under local law, nor who may issue its undertakings subject to the UCP. That restriction on the issuance of letters of credit is a regulatory matter under local law should be obvious. In some countries, non-banks can issue letters of credit, although there may be limitations where they are used in consumer situations. In other countries, issuance is limited to financial institutions, but it is less clear that only banks constitute financial institutions. As a result, non-banks that are financial institutions, such as insurance companies, can issue letters of credit in some countries.

It may be less apparent that the UCP cannot itself limit the scope of its application. The UCP is a set of voluntary rules of practice. The rules can be modified or excluded by the undertaking that is issued subject to them, as is recognized in UCP 500 Article 1 (Application of UCP) (The provisions 'are binding on all parties thereto, unless otherwise expressly stipulated in the Credit'). Issuance by a non-bank constitutes such a modification. Even if the UCP expressly prohibited issuance by a non-bank, this prohibition could be modified because the UCP is not a legislative act that can restrict the manner in which it can be applied.

Where a letter of credit is issued by a non-bank, the non-bank issuer should be held to the same obligation and standard of care as would a bank. In either case, the obligation is to pay against the presentation of documents that comply with the terms and conditions of the credit, and that determination is to be made based solely on the documentary presentation and not on the status of reimbursement obligations or the underlying transaction, and local law should apply the same principles to an independent undertaking regardless of who makes it.

Having concluded that a credit can be issued subject to the UCP by a non-bank, however, does not mean that it is prudent for a beneficiary to accept such a credit. Issuance through an advising bank does mitigate the issue of whether the credit is authentic and presentation of documents to a bank does reduce some operational risks. There is, nonetheless, the risk of the creditworthiness of the issuer and country risk.

These risks apply equally whether the issuer is or is not a bank, and a beneficiary should always assess whether it is prepared to accept the credit and country risk associated with the issuer. If not, it should require confirmation by an entity with which it is comfortable.

There remains, however, an additional risk that may not be apparent to beneficiaries, namely the risk of neutrality of the issuer. This risk is somewhat more intangible but is very important. It is the risk that, when presented with documents, the issuer may be influenced by factors other than whether they comply on their face with the terms and conditions of the credit and may exercise certain discretionary judgments in examining documents against the beneficiary where it would not otherwise do so if external factors were different. Whilst this risk is not confined to non-banks, the reputation of individual banks for integrity is well known in the letter of credit community and one which most banks that regularly engage in letter of credit practice work hard to maintain. It is less apparent that when faced with a poor credit decision, an insurance company will approach the problem in the same way as would a letter of credit banker rather than as an insurer, which may be inclined to reject all arguable claims and engage in litigation to settle any colourable dispute.

Similar concerns would apply to corporate issuers on behalf of themselves or affiliated companies, even though two-party letters of credit are recognized by UCP 500 Article 2 (Meaning of Credit) ('and on the instructions of a customer (the "Applicant") or on its own behalf').

For these reasons, it is generally in the interest of banks to inform corporate letter of credit users of the advantages of having a bank's obligation, either as the issuer of a credit or as the confirmer of a credit issued by a non-bank. There would be no objection under international standard letter of credit practice to informing specifically the beneficiary of such a credit as to the nature of the issuer in addition to emphasizing that the advising bank assumes no liability, although in the absence of agreed standards such a decision should rest with the individual bank involved.

Of course, where the manner of issuance misleads the beneficiary into believing that the issuer is a bank, the advising bank may expose itself to liability. Ultimately, however, the decision as to whether or not to accept the risks associated with a non-bank issuance rests with the beneficiary.

Conclusion

1. It does not 'violate' the UCP for a non-bank to issue a credit subject to the UCP, even though such issuance is not contemplated in the rules. The UCP does not specifically provide for bank advice of non-bank issued letters of credit. Such an advice should accurately identify the issuer and indicate the advising bank's limited role. If the form of advice refers to the 'issuer' as 'issuing bank' or otherwise gives the impression that it is a bank, it is recommended that the advice affirmatively disclose the non-bank status of the issuer in order to correct any mistaken impression caused by such reference.
2. The consequences of insolvency are a matter for local law, whether the insolvency is that of a bank or non-bank issuer. In either case, however, the beneficiary assumes the risk of the creditworthiness of the issuer unless it is offset by obtaining confirmation or credit insurance.

Negotiation

During the life of UCP 500, there was considerable discussion by the ICC Banking Commission concerning the meaning and proper use of negotiation as contained in sub-article 10 (b) (ii). This confusion principally centred on the use of the term "giving value". After UCP 500 was issued, ICC Position Paper No. 2 was published to try and clarify the use of negotiation and the definition in UCP 500. In addition, ICC Banking Commission Opinion TA 569 was issued to provide, amongst other points, a clear statement as to the structure of a documentary credit available by negotiation. The pertinent extract of the conclusion of this Opinion appears below:

> A letter of credit that is stated to be available with a nominated bank, by negotiation, should not include any reference to claiming reimbursement from a reimbursing bank or, indeed, any reference to the debiting of the issuing bank's account held with the nominated bank. This form of structure is a payment letter of credit. A negotiation letter of credit should specify that the nominated bank is to send the documents to the issuing bank, and upon the issuing bank ascertaining that it complies with the terms and conditions of the credit, the issuing bank will reimburse in accordance with the instructions of the negotiating bank.

UCP 600 has changed and simplified the definition to focus the concept on the purchase of drafts and/or documents by advancing, or agreeing to advance, funds to the beneficiary on or prior to the banking day that reimbursement is due.

In the definition of negotiation, the term "giving of value" has been substituted by the term "purchase". It is consistent with the statement in UCP 600 sub-article 12 (c) that examination and forwarding of documents do not constitute "negotiation". Under this definition, a nominated negotiating bank claiming reimbursement from an issuing bank or confirming bank under sub-articles 7 (c) or 8 (c) must have either advanced funds or agreed to do so. An agreement to advance funds if and when funds are received from the issuing bank is not "negotiation" under this definition. Accordingly, a bank nominated to negotiate may validly claim reimbursement according to the terms and conditions of the documentary credit after it undertakes to advance funds to the beneficiary by agreeing to a funding date set at or before the anticipated reimbursement date.

It should be noted that an issuing bank does not negotiate. When an issuing bank issues a documentary credit available by negotiation, a nominated bank acting on its nomination will negotiate, i.e., advance funds or agree to advance funds, but when the documents are received by the issuing bank they will either pay (a documentary credit available at sight with or without a draft), or accept or incur a deferred payment undertaking (a documentary credit available on usance terms with a draft (accept) or without a draft (incur a deferred payment undertaking)).

Nominated bank

"Nominated bank" was defined in UCP 500 in sub-article 10 (b) (i). UCP 600 has defined it to mean the bank with which the documentary credit is available, or any bank in the case of a documentary credit available with any bank. This new definition acknowledges, by the use of the term "available with any bank", the fact that a documentary credit can be made available by payment, acceptance, deferred payment or negotiation with any bank. The Drafting Group saw no reason why, with the correct structure with respect to the conditions for reimbursement, a credit available by payment, acceptance or deferred payment could not be made available with any bank, provided a reimbursing bank was authorized to honour a claim from any bank.

Presentation

The UCP 600 definition of "Presentation" contemplates two different uses of the term in the rules. The term must be read in the context in which it is used. The first use of the term refers to the actual delivery of the documents (physical presentation) to the bank; the second references the documents that have already been delivered to the bank and are in the bank's possession.

Presenter

The term "Presenter" has been introduced into UCP 600 to better define the party that actually makes a presentation of documents to the bank and to reference the party that presents the documents. The presenter may be either the beneficiary of the documentary credit, another bank or another party acting on behalf of the beneficiary. The definition of "Presenter" is particularly relevant under article 16 in relation to the sending of notices of refusal.

Cross-references within UCP 600

- The definitions contained in this article are used throughout UCP 600 and, as a result, the cross-references are too numerous to list.

ARTICLE 3

Interpretations

For the purpose of these rules:

Where applicable, words in the singular include the plural and in the plural include the singular.

A credit is irrevocable even if there is no indication to that effect.

A document may be signed by handwriting, facsimile signature, perforated signature, stamp, symbol or any other mechanical or electronic method of authentication.

A requirement for a document to be legalized, visaed, certified or similar will be satisfied by any signature, mark, stamp or label on the document which appears to satisfy that requirement.

Branches of a bank in different countries are considered to be separate banks.

Terms such as "first class", "well known", "qualified", "independent", "official", "competent" or "local" used to describe the issuer of a document allow any issuer except the beneficiary to issue that document.

Unless required to be used in a document, words such as "prompt", "immediately" or "as soon as possible" will be disregarded.

The expression "on or about" or similar will be interpreted as a stipulation that an event is to occur during a period of five calendar days before until five calendar days after the specified date, both start and end dates included.

The words "to", "until", "till", "from" and "between" when used to determine a period of shipment include the date or dates mentioned, and the words "before" and "after" exclude the date mentioned.

The words "from" and "after" when used to determine a maturity date exclude the date mentioned.

The terms "first half" and "second half" of a month shall be construed respectively as the 1st to the 15th and the 16th to the last day of the month, all dates inclusive.

The terms "beginning", "middle" and "end" of a month shall be construed respectively as the 1st to the 10th, the 11th to the 20th and the 21st to the last day of the month, all dates inclusive.

Changes from UCP 500

- New article to reflect the interpretations related to UCP.

Commentary

Article 3 of UCP 600 is a new article. The Drafting Group decided that, like definitions, the UCP would be simplified by putting all the concepts that it considered necessary to require interpretation in one article at the beginning of the rules. Each interpretation is discussed separately below.

Singular and plural – "Where applicable, words in the singular include the plural and in the plural include the singular."

Prior to UCP 600, depending on the context, terms were used in either the singular or plural or, where they could be used in both contexts, by including an (s) in the term. This usage made for difficult reading. The Drafting Group decided that the wording of the rules could be greatly simplified by using the singular and making the statement in the interpretations that "words in the singular include the plural and in the plural include the singular." Using this concept, it is important that terms used in the UCP be read in the context in which they are used, depending on the specific circumstances involved.

Irrevocability – "A credit is irrevocable even if there is no indication to that effect."

As used in UCP 600, reference to a documentary credit is always intended to mean an irrevocable documentary credit unless the documentary credit itself states otherwise, even if the documentary credit does not use the term irrevocable. Due to the limited use of revocable documentary credits today, they have been removed from UCP 600.

Signed – "A document may be signed by handwriting, facsimile signature, perforated signature, stamp, symbol or any other mechanical or electronic method of authentication."

This interpretation contains the general interpretation of what the terms "signed" and "signature" mean in the context of UCP 600. This interpretation was contained in UCP 500 sub-article 20 (b).

Legalization and certification – "A requirement for a document to be legalized, visaed, certified or similar will be satisfied by any signature, mark, stamp or label on the document which appears to satisfy that requirement."

Documents are often required to have some type of certification or legalization, and this interpretation states what will satisfy these requirements under the rules. This interpretation was contained in UCP 500 sub-article 20 (d).

Branches of banks – "Branches of a bank in different countries are considered to be separate banks."

It is often the case that branches of the same bank in different countries are involved in the same documentary credit transaction. Through the use of the term "separate banks", this interpretation makes it clear that for the purpose of these rules these branches of banks should be treated as separate banks. The interpretation contained in UCP 500 article 2 referred to such banks being "another bank". In the context of UCP they are not another bank, but they are a separate bank in relation to the functions they may perform under a documentary credit and the UCP.

From and after – "The words 'from' and 'after' when used to determine a maturity date exclude the date mentioned."

The interpretations of "from" and "after" as they specifically relate to maturity dates have been added to UCP 600. This interpretation originally appeared in ISBP, ICC Publication No. 645, in paragraph 45 (d). It should be noted that the interpretation of "from" in relation to maturity dates is different from that used in relation to periods for shipment.

General terminology and expressions

The remaining interpretations cover terms that are frequently used in documentary credits or documents and that have not essentially changed from those used in UCP 500. They provide guidance as to how the terms should be treated under the rules when used in documentary credit transactions. In general, they are self-explanatory. These interpretations are listed below simply for reference to their equivalent in UCP 500.

Terms such as "first class", "well known", "qualified", "independent", "official", "competent" or "local" used to describe the issuer of a document allow any issuer except the beneficiary to issue that document. This explanation was contained in UCP 500 sub-article 20 (a).

Unless required to be used in a document, words such as "prompt", "immediately" or "as soon as possible" will be disregarded. This explanation was contained in UCP 500 sub-article 46 (b) and ISBP, ICC Publication No. 645, paragraph 23.

The expression "on or about" or similar will be interpreted as a stipulation that an event is to occur during a period of five calendar days before until five calendar days after the specified date, both start and end dates included. This explanation was contained in UCP 500 sub-article 46 (c).

The words "to", "until", "till", "from" and "between" when used to determine a period of shipment include the date or dates mentioned, and the words "before" and "after" exclude the date mentioned. This explanation was contained in UCP 500 sub-article 47 (a).

The terms "first half" and "second half" of a month shall be construed respectively as the 1st to the 15th and the 16th to the last day of the month, all dates inclusive. This explanation was contained in UCP 500 sub-article 47 (c).

The terms "beginning", "middle" and "end" of a month shall be construed respectively as the 1st to the 10th, the 11th to the 20th and the 21st to the last day of the month, all dates inclusive. This explanation was contained in UCP 500 sub-article 47 (d).

Cross-references within UCP 600

- The interpretations contained in this article are used throughout UCP 600 in interpreting the rules and, as a result, the cross-references are too numerous to list.

ARTICLE 4

Credits v. Contracts

a. A credit by its nature is a separate transaction from the sale or other contract on which it may be based. Banks are in no way concerned with or bound by such contract, even if any reference whatsoever to it is included in the credit. Consequently, the undertaking of a bank to honour, to negotiate or to fulfil any other obligation under the credit is not subject to claims or defences by the applicant resulting from its relationships with the issuing bank or the beneficiary.

A beneficiary can in no case avail itself of the contractual relationships existing between banks or between the applicant and the issuing bank.

b. An issuing bank should discourage any attempt by the applicant to include, as an integral part of the credit, copies of the underlying contract, proforma invoice and the like.

CHANGES FROM UCP 500

- Use of the new term "honour";
- Addition of new sub-article (b) incorporating UCP 500 sub-article 5 (a) (i).

COMMENTARY

The essence of UCP 500 article 3 has been retained in UCP 600. The changes were made to incorporate the use of the singular and plural as articulated in article 3, as well as to incorporate the term "honour" as now defined in the rules.

The concept contained in UCP 500 sub-article 5(a) (i) concerning excessive detail has been incorporated into sub-article (b) and expanded. The current wording is stronger to discourage the incorporation of copies of contracts, proforma invoices, etc., as an integral part of a documentary credit. The Drafting Group recognized that there is nothing that can be stated in the rules that would prohibit a documentary credit from being issued with one or more of the attachments mentioned in this sub-article. An advising bank can elect not to a advise a documentary credit (sub-article 9 (e)), and if one or more of these attachments is included, this may be a reason for such an action. It should also be noted by applicants that the attaching of a proforma invoice or contract as an integral part of the documentary credit offers limited protection with regard to the goods and their standard or quality. Such issues are resolved by requiring the necessary documents and the data that is to appear therein.

Cross-references within UCP 600

- Article 2 – definitions of "Credit", "Honour", "Negotiate", "Applicant", "Issuing bank", "Beneficiary";
- Sub-article 9 (e), Advising of Credits and Amendments.

ARTICLE 5

Documents v. Goods, Services or Performance

Banks deal with documents and not with goods, services or performance to which the documents may relate.

CHANGES FROM UCP 500

- Change in title of the article;
- Deletion of reference to "In Credit Operations all parties concerned";
- Addition of "Banks";
- Change of "and/or other performances" to "or performance".

COMMENTARY

Several small changes have been made in this article. The title of the article has been changed from "Documents v. Goods/Services/Performances" to "Documents v. Goods, Services or Performance" to simplify the wording and to delete the use of a virgule ("/") between words.

UCP 500 article 4 stated: "In Credit operations all parties concerned deal with documents ...". The Drafting Group discussed the previous wording and decided that, in fact, in documentary credit operations all parties do not just deal with documents. The beneficiary of the documentary credit actually deals with the goods (services or performance), and as a result it was incorrect in the UCP to state that "all parties" do so. The article was changed to reflect the fact that banks deal with documents and not with the goods, services and performance to which the documents may relate.

To simplify the style in this article, as in others, the use of virgules has been eliminated and substituted simply by the use of "or performance".

CROSS-REFERENCES WITHIN UCP 600

None.

Article 6

Availability, Expiry Date and Place for Presentation

a. A credit must state the bank with which it is available or whether it is available with any bank. A credit available with a nominated bank is also available with the issuing bank.

b. A credit must state whether it is available by sight payment, deferred payment, acceptance or negotiation.

c. A credit must not be issued available by a draft drawn on the applicant.

d. i. A credit must state an expiry date for presentation. An expiry date stated for honour or negotiation will be deemed to be an expiry date for presentation.

ii. The place of the bank with which the credit is available is the place for presentation. The place for presentation under a credit available with any bank is that of any bank. A place for presentation other than that of the issuing bank is in addition to the place of the issuing bank.

e. Except as provided in sub-article 29 (a), a presentation by or on behalf of the beneficiary must be made on or before the expiry date.

Changes from UCP 500

- Introduction of freely available documentary credits as opposed to freely negotiable documentary credits;
- Sub-article (c) contains a stronger statement that drafts must not be drawn on the applicant;
- Clearer wording in sub-article (d) (i) for specifying the expiry date for presentation;
- Sub-article d (ii) details the rule for the place of presentation;
- Sub-article (e) states that presentation must be made on or before the expiry date;
- Article 6 refers to UCP 500 sub-articles 9 (a) (iv) and (b), 10 (a), 10 (b) (i), 42 (a) and 42 (b).

Commentary

UCP 600 article 6 details the rules for availability of the documentary credit, expiry date and place for presentation. Sub-article 6 (a) establishes the rule that a documentary credit must indicate the bank with which it is available or, in the case of a freely available documentary credit, that it is available with any bank. This sub-article widens the scope of the previous position in UCP 500 sub-article 10 (b) (i) stating that a documentary credit available by negotiation could be made "freely negotiable". Under UCP 600 a documentary credit can be issued on a "freely available" basis. Structured properly, a documentary credit can be made available with any bank for payment, acceptance or deferred payment – the three methods that make up the term "honour". Sub-article (a) also states the general rule that whilst a documentary credit may be made available with a nominated bank, it is always available with the issuing bank. As a result, a beneficiary always has the right to present documents either to the nominated bank or directly to the issuing bank.

Where UCP 600 article 2 defines "Honour" and states the methods of honour, sub-article (b) makes it clear that all documentary credits must specifically state the method of availability. Since a documentary credit cannot be made available by honour, it must state that it is available either by sight payment, deferred payment, acceptance or by negotiation.

UCP 500 sub-articles 9 (a) (iv) and (b) (iv) included the principle that documentary credits must not be made available by drafts drawn on the applicant. This rule is now affirmed in UCP 600 sub-article 6 (c). Whilst UCP 500 said that when a draft was to be drawn on the applicant it would be treated as an additional document, this has been deleted from UCP 600 to further reinforce the point that a documentary credit must not be made available by a draft drawn on the applicant. It should not be forgotten that a documentary credit constitutes an irrevocable undertaking of a bank. Having a documentary credit available by a draft drawn on the applicant can bring the applicant into the documentary credit settlement process and influence the point at which the issuing bank's undertaking comes into force, and thereby the timing in which the undertaking will be honoured.

Whilst sub-article 6 (c) states specifically that a documentary credit must not be made available by a draft drawn on the applicant, it is possible for a documentary credit to demand a draft drawn on the applicant as a required document under the documentary credit. This draft would be treated as any other required document, and it would be necessary for the issuing bank to specifically indicate the requirements and content for such a draft.

Sub-article (d) (i) specifically states that all documentary credits must have an expiry date and that an expiry date indicated for honour or negotiation is an expiry date for presentation. This statement is the equivalent of that found in UCP 500 sub-article 42 (a).

Sub-article (d) (ii) further clarifies the rule in sub-article (a) that the place where the documentary credit is available is the place for presentation. If the documentary credit is available with any bank, the place for presentation is at the bank to which presentation is made by the beneficiary or other presenter. A place for presentation stated in the documentary credit is always in addition to the place of the issuing bank.

A beneficiary electing to present documents directly to an issuing bank should be aware that sub-article (d) (ii) does not imply an extension of the expiry date or any presentation period as indicated in sub-article 14 (c), or one that may be indicated in the documentary credit. It should be noted that in such circumstances the beneficiary is responsible for delivery of documents to the issuing bank. Any loss due to a delay in the issuing bank's receiving the documents, or the documents' being lost in transit, would be the responsibility of the beneficiary.

Sub-article (e) is essentially the same as UCP 500 sub-article 42 (b), indicating that presentation must be made on or before the expiry date of the documentary credit. Additional language was added so that "presentation by or on behalf of the beneficiary" allows presentation by someone other than the beneficiary that is acting on its behalf, such as another bank or freight forwarder.

Cross-references within UCP 600

- Article 2 – definition of "Honour", "Negotiation", "Complying presentation", "Presentation" and "Presenter";
- Articles 7 on undertaking of the issuing bank;
- Article 8 on undertaking of the confirming bank;
- Sub-article 14 (c) on presentation of documents;
- Sub-articles 15 (b) and (c) on forwarding of documents by a confirming bank or nominated bank;
- Sub-article 29 (a) on extension of the period for presentation.

ARTICLE 7

Issuing Bank Undertaking

a. Provided that the stipulated documents are presented to the nominated bank or to the issuing bank and that they constitute a complying presentation, the issuing bank must honour if the credit is available by:

  i. sight payment, deferred payment or acceptance with the issuing bank;

  ii. sight payment with a nominated bank and that nominated bank does not pay;

  iii. deferred payment with a nominated bank and that nominated bank does not incur its deferred payment undertaking or, having incurred its deferred payment undertaking, does not pay at maturity;

  iv. acceptance with a nominated bank and that nominated bank does not accept a draft drawn on it or, having accepted a draft drawn on it, does not pay at maturity;

  v. negotiation with a nominated bank and that nominated bank does not negotiate.

b. An issuing bank is irrevocably bound to honour as of the time it issues the credit.

c. An issuing bank undertakes to reimburse a nominated bank that has honoured or negotiated a complying presentation and forwarded the documents to the issuing bank. Reimbursement for the amount of a complying presentation under a credit available by acceptance or deferred payment is due at maturity, whether or not the nominated bank prepaid or purchased before maturity. An issuing bank's undertaking to reimburse a nominated bank is independent of the issuing bank's undertaking to the beneficiary.

CHANGES FROM UCP 500

- New structure as a result of the definition of "Honour";
- A statement that an issuing bank is bound as of the time it issues the documentary credit;
- A clarification that an issuing bank undertakes to reimburse a nominated bank that has honoured, whether or not the nominated bank prepaid or purchased;
- Article 7 refers to UCP 500 article 2 and sub-articles 9 (a), 10 (d) and 14 (a).

Commentary

UCP 600 sub-article 7 (a) is the equivalent of UCP 500 sub-articles 9 (a) (i) to (iv) and has been rewritten due to the introduction of "Honour" and to reflect the use of the new UCP 600 article 2 definitions of "Beneficiary", "Complying presentation", "Credit", "Issuing bank", "Negotiation" and "Nominated bank". The use of these definitions has allowed the article to become more concise and easier to read.

Sub-article (a) states the basic rule that an issuing bank's undertaking is to honour a presentation that complies with the terms and conditions of the documentary credit when the documents are presented to the nominated bank or the issuing bank. The specific methods of honour are articulated in sub-articles (a) (i) to (v). The sub-article states that honour is to be effected by the issuing bank when the documentary credit is only available with the issuing bank or when the presenter chooses to make a presentation directly to the issuing bank (sub-article (a) (i)) or, in the event that a nominated bank does not honour, (sub-articles (a) (ii), (iii) and (iv)). Sub-article (v) states that the issuing bank will honour if the documentary credit is available by negotiation and the nominated bank does not negotiate.

An issuing bank does not negotiate its own documentary credit; it honours by paying at sight, accepting a draft drawn on it and paying at maturity or by incurring a deferred payment undertaking and paying at maturity.

Sub-article (b) states that the issuing bank is irrevocably bound to honour as of the time it issues the documentary credit. This wording is new to the UCP. UCP 500 sub-article 9 (d) (ii) stated that the issuing bank was irrevocably bound as of the time of issuance of an amendment to the documentary credit; however, the UCP did not state specifically that the issuing bank was bound to honour its documentary credit as of the time of issuance.

Sub-article 7 (c) expressly recognizes that an issuing bank's obligation to reimburse a nominated bank is separate and independent of its obligation to honour a beneficiary's presentation for honour. This sub-article is consistent with the express authority in sub-article 12 (b) for a nominated bank to prepay (and discharge) or purchase (and either resell or hold to maturity) its obligation. Reimbursement under this sub-article becomes due at maturity in all cases, including when prepayment or purchase has been effected.

Cross-references within UCP 600

- Article 2 – definitions of "Beneficiary", "Complying presentation", "Credit", "Honour", "Issuing bank", "Negotiation" and "Nominated bank";
- Article 8 on liability of the confirming bank;
- Article 12 on liability of a nominated bank;
- Article 12 on authorization for the nominated bank to prepay or purchase;
- Article 15 on complying presentation;
- Article 15 on the confirming and nominated banks' obligation to forward documents.

ARTICLE 8

Confirming Bank Undertaking

a. Provided that the stipulated documents are presented to the confirming bank or to any other nominated bank and that they constitute a complying presentation, the confirming bank must:

   i. honour, if the credit is available by

      a) sight payment, deferred payment or acceptance with the confirming bank;

      b) sight payment with another nominated bank and that nominated bank does not pay;

      c) deferred payment with another nominated bank and that nominated bank does not incur its deferred payment undertaking or, having incurred its deferred payment undertaking, does not pay at maturity;

      d) acceptance with another nominated bank and that nominated bank does not accept a draft drawn on it or, having accepted a draft drawn on it, does not pay at maturity;

      e) negotiation with another nominated bank and that nominated bank does not negotiate.

   ii. negotiate, without recourse, if the credit is available by negotiation with the confirming bank.

b. A confirming bank is irrevocably bound to honour or negotiate as of the time it adds its confirmation to the credit.

c. A confirming bank undertakes to reimburse another nominated bank that has honoured or negotiated a complying presentation and forwarded the documents to the confirming bank. Reimbursement for the amount of a complying presentation under a credit available by acceptance or deferred payment is due at maturity, whether or not another nominated bank prepaid or purchased before maturity. A confirming bank's undertaking to reimburse another nominated bank is independent of the confirming bank's undertaking to the beneficiary.

d. If a bank is authorized or requested by the issuing bank to confirm a credit but is not prepared to do so, it must inform the issuing bank without delay and may advise the credit without confirmation.

Changes from UCP 500

- New structure as a result of the definition of "Honour";
- A statement that a confirming bank is bound as of the time it confirms the documentary credit;
- A clarification that a confirming bank undertakes to reimburse another nominated bank that has honoured or negotiated whether or not the nominated bank prepaid or purchased;
- Article 8 refers to UCP 500 sub-articles 9 (b) and (c) and 14 (a).

Commentary

UCP 600 sub-article 8 (a) is the equivalent of UCP 500 sub-article 9 (b) (i) to (iv) and has been rewritten due to the introduction of "Honour" and to reflect the use of the new UCP 600 article 2 definitions of "Beneficiary", "Complying presentation", "Confirming bank", "Credit", "Negotiation" and "Nominated bank". The use of these definitions has allowed the article to become more concise and easier to read.

Sub-article (a) states the basic rule that a confirming bank's undertaking is to honour a presentation that complies with the terms and conditions of the documentary credit when the documents are presented to any other nominated bank or the confirming bank. The specific methods of honour are articulated in sub-articles (a) (i) (a) to (e). The sub-article states that honour is to be effected by the confirming bank when the documentary credit is only available with the confirming bank or when the presenter makes a presentation directly to the confirming bank (sub-article (a) (i) (a)) or, in the event that a nominated bank does not honour, (sub-article (a) (i) (b), (c) and (d). Sub-article (a) (i) (e) states that the confirming bank will honour if the documentary credit is available by negotiation with another nominated bank and that nominated bank does not negotiate.

Sub-article (a) (ii) addresses the circumstance in which the documentary credit is available with the confirming bank by negotiation and the undertaking of the confirming bank is to negotiate. A confirming bank that negotiates does so on a without recourse basis.

Sub-article (b) states that the confirming bank is irrevocably bound to honour as of the time it confirms the documentary credit. This wording is new to the UCP.

Sub-article 8 (c) is the equivalent of UCP 500 sub-article 14 (a) and expressly recognizes that a confirming bank's obligation to reimburse a nominated bank is separate and independent of its obligation to honour a beneficiary's presentation for honour. This sub-article is consistent with the express authority in sub-article 12 (b) for a nominated bank to prepay (and discharge) or purchase (and either resell or hold to maturity) its obligation. Reimbursement under this sub-article becomes due at maturity in all cases, including when prepayment or purchase has been effected.

Sub-article 8 (d) restates the principle contained in the second part of UCP 500 sub-article 9 (d) (ii) that a confirming bank may choose not to add its confirmation provided that it informs the issuing bank of its action, and it may advise the documentary credit without confirmation.

Cross-references within UCP 600

- Article 2 – definitions of "Beneficiary", "Complying presentation", "Credit", "Honour", "Issuing bank", "Negotiation" and "Nominated bank";
- Article 8 on liability of confirming bank;
- Article 12 on liability of a nominated bank;
- Article 12 on authorization for the nominated bank to prepay or purchase;
- Article 15 on complying presentation;
- Article 15 on the confirming and nominated banks' obligation to forward documents.

ARTICLE 9

Advising of Credits and Amendments

a. A credit and any amendment may be advised to a beneficiary through an advising bank. An advising bank that is not a confirming bank advises the credit and any amendment without any undertaking to honour or negotiate.

b. By advising the credit or amendment, the advising bank signifies that it has satisfied itself as to the apparent authenticity of the credit or amendment and that the advice accurately reflects the terms and conditions of the credit or amendment received.

c. An advising bank may utilize the services of another bank ("second advising bank") to advise the credit and any amendment to the beneficiary. By advising the credit or amendment, the second advising bank signifies that it has satisfied itself as to the apparent authenticity of the advice it has received and that the advice accurately reflects the terms and conditions of the credit or amendment received.

d. A bank utilizing the services of an advising bank or second advising bank to advise a credit must use the same bank to advise any amendment thereto.

e. If a bank is requested to advise a credit or amendment but elects not to do so, it must so inform, without delay, the bank from which the credit, amendment or advice has been received.

f. If a bank is requested to advise a credit or amendment but cannot satisfy itself as to the apparent authenticity of the credit, the amendment or the advice, it must so inform, without delay, the bank from which the instructions appear to have been received. If the advising bank or second advising bank elects nonetheless to advise the credit or amendment, it must inform the beneficiary or second advising bank that it has not been able to satisfy itself as to the apparent authenticity of the credit, the amendment or the advice.

CHANGES FROM UCP 500

- New article;
- Removal of the term "without engagement";
- Change in the concept of "reasonable care" as to the apparent authenticity of the advice;
- Introduction of the principle of the accuracy of the advice;
- Introduction of the concept of a second advising bank.

Commentary

This new article consolidates the concepts of UCP 500 article 7 and sub-article 11 (b) into one article covering the advice of documentary credits and amendments.

Sub-article (a) removes the prior concept of "without engagement" and replaces it with the term "without any undertaking" to better differentiate the undertaking of the issuing bank from the fact that the advising bank has no undertaking to honour or negotiate.

Sub-article (b) addresses two responsibilities for the advising bank: first, that it has satisfied itself as to the apparent authenticity of the documentary credit or amendment; and second, that its advice accurately reflects the terms and conditions of the documentary credit or amendment received. UCP 500 used the often-misunderstood concept that the advising bank should exercise reasonable care in establishing the apparent authenticity of the documentary credit. By changing the concept to one where the advising bank must satisfy itself as to the apparent authenticity, the new provision aligns itself more closely with the standard practices of banks as to what they actually do in authenticating a documentary credit or amendment.

The concept of the advice accurately reflecting the terms and conditions of the documentary credit has been added to emphasize the responsibility of the advising bank for ensuring that the documentary credit or amendment sent to it by the issuing bank is accurately advised by it to the second advising bank or to the beneficiary. To satisfy the requirement of the "advice accurately reflecting", the advising bank or second advising bank is responsible for ensuring that what is received by it – at a minimum, the information pertinent for the beneficiary to perform under the documentary credit – is advised to the beneficiary. Documentary credits often include information that can be classed as "bank-to-bank information", such as refinancing requests, credit agreements and specific instructions for the nominated bank. These pieces of information may be extracted or deleted from the advice conveyed to the beneficiary.

Sub-article (c) introduces the concept of a second advising bank. Whilst the use of, and reference to, a second advising bank has been practice for a number of years, the UCP never previously acknowledged its role. The new sub-article states that the second advising bank has much the same role as the advising bank in satisfying itself as to the apparent authenticity of the advice that it has received from the advising bank, and that its advice of the documentary credit or amendment accurately reflects the advice of the documentary credit or amendment received from the advising bank.

UCP 500 stated the principle contained in UCP 600 sub-article (d) in UCP 500 sub-article 11 (b). The rule has been moved to this article so as to include in one place all of the rules related to advising a documentary credit or amendment. This rule ensures that the chain of communication between the parties will be maintained, not only for the advising of the documentary credit, but also for any amendments thereto.

Sub-articles (e) and (f) articulate the same principles contained in UCP 500 sub-articles 7 (a) and (b) when the advising bank or second advising bank is unable to satisfy itself as to the apparent authenticity of the documentary credit or amendment. Whilst these sub-articles provide for such a bank to advise the documentary credit or amendment without satisfying itself as to its apparent authenticity, most banks will normally seek proper authentication from the issuing bank.

Cross-references within UCP 600

- Article 2 – definitions of "Advising bank", "Honour" and "Negotiate".

Article 10

Amendments

a. Except as otherwise provided by article 38, a credit can neither be amended nor cancelled without the agreement of the issuing bank, the confirming bank, if any, and the beneficiary.

b. An issuing bank is irrevocably bound by an amendment as of the time it issues the amendment. A confirming bank may extend its confirmation to an amendment and will be irrevocably bound as of the time it advises the amendment. A confirming bank may, however, choose to advise an amendment without extending its confirmation and, if so, it must inform the issuing bank without delay and inform the beneficiary in its advice.

c. The terms and conditions of the original credit (or a credit incorporating previously accepted amendments) will remain in force for the beneficiary until the beneficiary communicates its acceptance of the amendment to the bank that advised such amendment. The beneficiary should give notification of acceptance or rejection of an amendment. If the beneficiary fails to give such notification, a presentation that complies with the credit and to any not yet accepted amendment will be deemed to be notification of acceptance by the beneficiary of such amendment. As of that moment the credit will be amended.

d. A bank that advises an amendment should inform the bank from which it received the amendment of any notification of acceptance or rejection.

e. Partial acceptance of an amendment is not allowed and will be deemed to be notification of rejection of the amendment.

f. A provision in an amendment to the effect that the amendment shall enter into force unless rejected by the beneficiary within a certain time shall be disregarded.

Changes from UCP 500

- Notification of acceptance or rejection;
- Definitive statement that partial acceptance will be deemed rejection;
- Time limits for amendments will be disregarded when imposing acceptance.

Commentary

Sub-articles 10 (a), (b) and (c) contain the concepts of UCP 500 sub-articles 9 (d) (i), (ii) and (iii) with only slight modifications for changes in style and to reflect defined terms.

During the course of the revision, several options for the determination of acceptance or rejection of amendments contained in sub-article (c) were provided to ICC national committees. These included what probably would be the most definitive way to determine whether or not the beneficiary had accepted or rejected an amendment, i.e., that the beneficiary was required to advise the advising bank and/or the nominated bank no later than the date of presentation of the documents which amendments had been accepted or rejected. These options were not accepted in favour of continuing with the principles contained in UCP 500 sub-article 9 (d) (iii).

Sub-article (d) addresses the instance in which an advising bank or second advising bank may receive a notification of acceptance or rejection on or prior to presentation of the documents and states that the advising or second advising bank should inform the bank from which it received the amendment of any acceptance or rejection received prior to presentation.

The wording of sub-article (e) has been changed from that contained in UCP 500 sub-article 9 (d) (iv) to provide a more definitive statement that partial acceptance will be deemed to be a rejection.

Sub-article (f) is new to the UCP and addresses the issues contained in Position Paper No. 1 issued by ICC in relation to UCP 500. The position paper addressed the situation in which amendments were being issued that included wording to the effect that the amendment will be deemed to have been accepted by the beneficiary unless rejected by it within a specified time period. This practice was felt to restrict the rights of a beneficiary in deciding when to either accept or reject an amendment to a documentary credit. The new rule states that such conditions in an amendment will be disregarded.

Cross-references within UCP 600

- Article 2 – definitions of "Beneficiary", "Presentation", "Advising bank", "Issuing bank" and "Nominated bank";
- Article 38 – Transferable Credits.

Article 11

Teletransmitted and Pre-Advised Credits and Amendments

a. An authenticated teletransmission of a credit or amendment will be deemed to be the operative credit or amendment, and any subsequent mail confirmation shall be disregarded.

If a teletransmission states "full details to follow" (or words of similar effect), or states that the mail confirmation is to be the operative credit or amendment, then the teletransmission will not be deemed to be the operative credit or amendment. The issuing bank must then issue the operative credit or amendment without delay in terms not inconsistent with the teletransmission.

b. A preliminary advice of the issuance of a credit or amendment ("pre-advice") shall only be sent if the issuing bank is prepared to issue the operative credit or amendment. An issuing bank that sends a pre-advice is irrevocably committed to issue the operative credit or amendment, without delay, in terms not inconsistent with the pre-advice.

Changes from UCP 500

- A mail confirmation of an authenticated teletransmission of a documentary credit shall be disregarded;
- Obligation to issue the documentary credit not inconsistent with the terms of the teletransmission;
- Removal of reference to irrevocable credit based on the definition of "Credit".

Commentary

Article 11 is essentially the same as UCP 500 sub-articles 11 (a) and (c). UCP 500 sub-article 11 (b) has now been moved to UCP 600 sub-article 9 (d).

Sub-article (a) has been modified to state a more definitive rule that an authenticated teletransmission will be deemed to be the operative documentary credit or amendment, and should a mail confirmation be sent, it will be disregarded. If an issuing bank issues a documentary credit on the basis that it is not to be deemed to be the operative documentary credit or amendment, then it must clearly indicate this fact by use of wording such as "full details to follow" or similar. When such an advice is issued, the issuing bank must issue the operative documentary credit or amendment in terms not inconsistent with the teletransmission and without delay.

Sub-article (b) has been modified to remove the reference to irrevocable credit, since this is now included in the definition of "Credit" in article 2.

Cross-references within UCP 600

- Article 2 – definition of "Credit".

Article 12

Nomination

a. Unless a nominated bank is the confirming bank, an authorization to honour or negotiate does not impose any obligation on that nominated bank to honour or negotiate, except when expressly agreed to by that nominated bank and so communicated to the beneficiary.

b. By nominating a bank to accept a draft or incur a deferred payment undertaking, an issuing bank authorizes that nominated bank to prepay or purchase a draft accepted or a deferred payment undertaking incurred by that nominated bank.

c. Receipt or examination and forwarding of documents by a nominated bank that is not a confirming bank does not make that nominated bank liable to honour or negotiate, nor does it constitute honour or negotiation.

Changes from UCP 500

- Aligning of defined terms in article 2;
- Addition of express authorization for a nominated bank to prepay or purchase its own accepted draft or deferred payment undertaking.

Commentary

Sub-article (a) is similar to UCP 500 sub-article 10 (c). Nominating a bank to honour or negotiate does not obligate that bank to receive or examine documents or to honour or negotiate unless the nominated bank is the confirming bank of the documentary credit, or when the nominated bank expressly communicates its agreement to honour or negotiate to the beneficiary, i.e., by indicating that it is willing to act under its nomination. It should be noted that, subject to the structure of the documentary credit, a confirming bank may not be a nominated bank.

Sub-article (b) is new to the UCP. This sub-article provides within the rules that any nominated bank is automatically authorized to prepay or purchase a draft accepted by it and to prepay or purchase a deferred payment undertaking incurred by it. This provision recognizes the independent, absolute and unconditional nature of a nominated bank's obligation under its own accepted draft or incurred deferred payment undertaking. It thus responds to legal questions raised as to whether UCP 500 or international standard banking practice supports discounting of such obligations by nominated bank obligors.

With this new sub-article, the rules provide for discount authorization simply by the issuing bank nominating a bank to accept a draft or incur a deferred payment undertaking. A bank nominated to negotiate is, by the definition of "negotiation" in UCP 600, as well as UCP 500, authorized to purchase a complying presentation (under UCP 500 to "give value").

There is now no difference between the authorization to prepay or purchase a draft accepted or deferred payment undertaking incurred by a nominated bank and the authorization to negotiate, i.e., to purchase a complying presentation.

Sub-article (c) states the same principle as that found in the second sentence of UCP 500 sub-article 10 (b) (ii) that receipt, examination and forwarding of documents does not constitute negotiation (or honour) or obligate a nominated bank to honour or negotiate.

Cross-references within UCP 600

- Definitions of "Nominated bank", "Confirming bank", "Honour", "Negotiate", "Beneficiary" and "Applicant";
- Sub-article 7 (c);
- Sub-article 8 (c);
- Sub-articles 16 (a), (c) and (e) regarding the nominated bank acting on its nomination.

ARTICLE 13

Bank-to-Bank Reimbursement Arrangements

a. If a credit states that reimbursement is to be obtained by a nominated bank ("claiming bank") claiming on another party ("reimbursing bank"), the credit must state if the reimbursement is subject to the ICC rules for bank-to-bank reimbursements in effect on the date of issuance of the credit.

b. If a credit does not state that reimbursement is subject to the ICC rules for bank-to-bank reimbursements, the following apply:

  i. An issuing bank must provide a reimbursing bank with a reimbursement authorization that conforms with the availability stated in the credit. The reimbursement authorization should not be subject to an expiry date.

  ii. A claiming bank shall not be required to supply a reimbursing bank with a certificate of compliance with the terms and conditions of the credit.

  iii. An issuing bank will be responsible for any loss of interest, together with any expenses incurred, if reimbursement is not provided on first demand by a reimbursing bank in accordance with the terms and conditions of the credit.

  iv. A reimbursing bank's charges are for the account of the issuing bank. However, if the charges are for the account of the beneficiary, it is the responsibility of an issuing bank to so indicate in the credit and in the reimbursement authorization. If a reimbursing bank's charges are for the account of the beneficiary, they shall be deducted from the amount due to a claiming bank when reimbursement is made. If no reimbursement is made, the reimbursing bank's charges remain the obligation of the issuing bank.

c. An issuing bank is not relieved of any of its obligations to provide reimbursement if reimbursement is not made by a reimbursing bank on first demand.

Changes from UCP 500

- Alignment of the article with the *Uniform Rules for Bank-to-Bank Reimbursements* (URR);
- Incorporation of the URR into the documentary credit;
- Deletion of the term "good time";
- Introduction of no expiry date;
- Stronger treatment of the issuing bank's responsibility for charges.

Commentary

Since the ICC's *Uniform Rules for Bank-to-Bank Reimbursements* ("URR") (ICC Publication No. 525) were issued after the implementation of UCP 500, the revision of the UCP provided the first opportunity to bring the UCP into conformity with those rules. One of the basic questions posed to the Drafting Group was whether the URR should be incorporated into the UCP, thereby eliminating the need for a separate set of rules. The international standby rules (ISP98) in rule 8.04, Bank-to-Bank Reimbursement, state: "Any instruction or authorization to obtain reimbursement from another bank is subject to the International Chamber of Commerce standard rules for bank-to-bank reimbursements." As a result, and given the fact that the URR will need to be updated, there continues to be the need for the URR to remain a separate set of rules. Consequently, the Drafting Group decided not to incorporate the URR into the UCP, but to bring article 13 into conformity with the URR.

Following the same concept used in ISP98, sub-article 13 (a) has been changed to state that if the documentary credit indicates that reimbursement is to be obtained from a reimbursing bank, it must indicate if the reimbursement is subject to the ICC rules for bank-to-bank reimbursements. The generic term "ICC rules for bank-to-bank reimbursements" has been used in both UCP 600 and ISP98, rather than having a specific reference to the current ICC publication (ICC Publication No. 525). In this way, if the reimbursement rules change in the future, it will not cause a conflict with the UCP.

If the documentary credit states that it is subject to the URR, those rules will apply to the reimbursement. Should the documentary credit not state that it is subject to the URR, as indicated in sub-article (a), sub-article (b) of article 13 will apply to the reimbursement.

The remainder of the article contains the same rules as UCP 500 with a few changes to bring them more in line with the URR.

Sub-article (b) (i) states that the reimbursement should not be subject to any expiry date, a similar position to that in the URR. In addition, the sub-article asserts that the reimbursement should conform to the availability stated in the documentary credit.

Sub-article (b) (ii) reflects the same principle as in UCP 500 sub-article 19 (b) from a slightly different perspective. It states that a claiming bank shall not be required to supply a certificate of compliance, whereas UCP 500 says that the issuing bank should not require a certificate of compliance.

Sub-article (b) (iv) brings the subject of charges in line with the URR by stating in stronger words that reimbursement charges are for the account of the issuing bank. It further states that should the charges not be for the account of the issuing bank, they may be deducted from the proceeds of the reimbursement.

Sub-article (c) applies to both sub-article 13 (a) and 13 (b) and contains the same principle as in UCP 500, namely that an issuing bank is not relieved of its obligation to provide reimbursement should the reimbursement not be made by the reimbursing bank.

Cross-references within UCP 600

- Article 2 – Definitions.

ARTICLE 14

Standard for Examination of Documents

a. A nominated bank acting on its nomination, a confirming bank, if any, and the issuing bank must examine a presentation to determine, on the basis of the documents alone, whether or not the documents appear on their face to constitute a complying presentation.

b. A nominated bank acting on its nomination, a confirming bank, if any, and the issuing bank shall each have a maximum of five banking days following the day of presentation to determine if a presentation is complying. This period is not curtailed or otherwise affected by the occurrence on or after the date of presentation of any expiry date or last day for presentation.

c. A presentation including one or more original transport documents subject to articles 19, 20, 21, 22, 23, 24 or 25 must be made by or on behalf of the beneficiary not later than 21 calendar days after the date of shipment as described in these rules, but in any event not later than the expiry date of the credit.

d. Data in a document, when read in context with the credit, the document itself and international standard banking practice, need not be identical to, but must not conflict with, data in that document, any other stipulated document or the credit.

e. In documents other than the commercial invoice, the description of the goods, services or performance, if stated, may be in general terms not conflicting with their description in the credit.

f. If a credit requires presentation of a document other than a transport document, insurance document or commercial invoice, without stipulating by whom the document is to be issued or its data content, banks will accept the document as presented if its content appears to fulfil the function of the required document and otherwise complies with sub-article 14 (d).

g. A document presented but not required by the credit will be disregarded and may be returned to the presenter.

h. If a credit contains a condition without stipulating the document to indicate compliance with the condition, banks will deem such condition as not stated and will disregard it.

i. A document may be dated prior to the issuance date of the credit, but must not be dated later than its date of presentation.

j. When the addresses of the beneficiary and the applicant appear in any stipulated document, they need not be the same as those stated in the credit or in any other stipulated document, but must be within the same country as the respective addresses mentioned in the credit. Contact details (telefax, telephone, email and the like) stated as part of the beneficiary's and the applicant's address will be disregarded. However, when the address and contact details of the applicant appear as part of the consignee or notify party details on a transport document subject to articles 19, 20, 21, 22, 23, 24 or 25, they must be as stated in the credit.

k. The shipper or consignor of the goods indicated on any document need not be the beneficiary of the credit.

l. A transport document may be issued by any party other than a carrier, owner, master or charterer provided that the transport document meets the requirements of articles 19, 20, 21, 22, 23 or 24 of these rules.

Changes from UCP 500

- Sub-article 14 (a) combines UCP 500 sub-articles 13 (a) and 14 (b);
- A shorter period of time for examination of documents;
- The period for examination of documents is independent of forthcoming events or time lines;
- Sub-article 14 (b) refers to UCP 500 sub-article 13 (b);
- The default presentation period applies to presentations that include an original transport document;
- Sub-article 14 (c) combines UCP 500 sub-article 43 (a) and ISBP, ICC Publication No. 645, paragraph 16;
- Data must not be in "conflict" rather than not being "inconsistent";
- Sub-article 14 (d) refers to UCP 500 sub-article 13 (a);
- Description of goods, services or performance must not be in "conflict" rather than not being "inconsistent";
- Sub-article 14 (e) refers to UCP 500 sub-article 37 (c);
- For documents other than transport documents, insurance documents or commercial invoices, the documentary credit must specify their data content; otherwise, such documents must appear to fulfil the function of the named document;

- Sub-article 14 (f) refers to UCP 500 article 21;
- Sub-article 14 (g) refers to UCP 500 sub-article 13 (a);
- Sub-article 14 (h) of UCP 600 refers to UCP 500 sub-article 13 (c) and includes the concept contained in UCP 500 sub-article 5 (b), which is no longer explicitly stated;
- Sub-article 14 (i) refers to UCP 500 article 22;
- Except in certain limited cases, differences in the addresses and contact details of the beneficiary and the applicant from those stated in a credit are to be disregarded;
- Sub-article 14 (j) refers to ISBP, ICC Publication No. 645, paragraphs 60 and 61;
- Sub-article 14 (k) refers to UCP 500 sub-article 31 (c) (iii), widening the scope to cover any document;
- Sub-article 14 (l) refers to UCP 500 article 30.

COMMENTARY

During the course of the revision, the Drafting Group decided that, based on the number of queries received by the Banking Commission during the life of UCP 500, further clarification was needed with regard to UCP 500 articles 13 (Standard for Examination of Documents) and 14 (Discrepant Documents and Notice). As a result, UCP 600 article 14 on Standard for Examination of Documents introduces a new structure by setting the standards by which banks should approach the examination of documents and has been significantly expanded to capture the specific requirements applicable to all or most documents contained in a presentation. These requirements are in addition to those outlined in the specific articles covering transport documents, insurance documents and commercial invoices.

Sub-article 14 (a) establishes the basic rule that the issuing bank, confirming bank, if any, and a nominated bank acting on its nomination must examine a presentation based on the documents alone to determine if, on their face, they constitute a complying presentation. It is the equivalent of UCP 500 sub-articles 13 (a) and 14 (b). This stance within the UCP has been well established and has been modified only slightly to incorporate the UCP 600-defined term "Complying presentation".

Whilst the phrase "on their face" continues to remain in this article, it has been removed from all other articles of UCP 600. The phrase, as it is used in relation to the examination of documents, was seen to be a well-established concept understood by those in the legal profession and experienced documentary credit practitioners. The concept of "on their face" does not refer to a simple front versus the back of a document, but extends to the review of data within a document in order to determine that a presentation complies with international standard banking practice and the principles contained in UCP. Because the term remained in the UCP in relation to the examination of documents in general, the Drafting Group did not see any reason to repeat it in other articles, such as the transport, insurance and commercial invoice articles, as was the case in UCP 500. Banks are not obliged to go beyond the face of a document to establish whether or not a document complies with a requirement in a documentary credit or with any requirement in the UCP.

As a general rule, this sub-article applies to the examination of all documents presented under a credit.

Sub-article 14 (a) differs from UCP 500 article 13 in that, as a result of the use of the definition of "Complying presentation", it requires that a presentation comply with the terms and conditions of a documentary credit, which includes complying with the terms of UCP 600 indicated in the documentary credit, which in turn includes being in accord with international standard banking practice. The requirement to use "reasonable care" has been removed and has been superseded by these more comprehensive and precise requirements. This change is prompted also by the progress made since UCP 500 was published in documenting international standard banking practice as applied to the examination of most documents presented under documentary credits, notably in ICC Publication No. 645 (2003) and the updated ICC Publication No. 681 for use with UCP 600.

A nominated bank (that is not obligated as a confirming bank) may "act on its nomination" by express agreement as provided in sub-article 12 (a), or by examining the presentation for compliance with the documentary credit and, in most countries, charging a fee. Receipt of documents by a nominated bank that has neither expressly agreed to honour nor negotiate a complying presentation, nor acted on its nomination, constitutes presentation by the beneficiary under the documentary credit, but does not obligate the nominated bank to observe the provisions of sub-articles 14 (a) or (b).

UCP 600 sub-article 14 (b) establishes the maximum period of time for the examination of documents to be five banking days following the day of presentation in order to determine if a presentation is complying and differs in several important respects from UCP 500 sub-article 13 (b). In addition to the fact that the time period has been reduced from seven to five banking days following the day of presentation, the reference to "reasonable time" has been removed. Reference to reasonable time was removed from UCP 600 due to the lack of a standard application of this concept globally. In fact, it was still the case during the revision process that a number of banks considered a reasonable time to be the full seven banking days following the day of receipt of the documents. The majority of ICC national committees voted for the removal of the reference to "reasonable time".

The sub-article now sets out the period of time as a maximum of five banking days following the day of presentation to establish the maximum period for determination of compliance. The period of five banking days following the day of presentation was determined following consultation with ICC national committees, when they were asked to vote for the applicable number of days, taking into consideration that agreement had already been reached to remove a reference to "reasonable time".

The second part of the sub-article is new to the UCP and states that the maximum period of time for determining compliance is not curtailed or affected by the date of expiry or latest date for presentation of the documentary credit falling within this period. Banks process presentations within the normal flow of business transactions and are not responsible for expediting examination because the documentary credit is about to expire. It is the responsibility of the beneficiary to ensure that documents are presented in sufficient time so that if there are correctable discrepancies, it may have the time to correct these and re-present the documents.

Sub-article (c) states that if a presentation includes an original transport document (those subject to the transport articles of the UCP, namely articles 19–25), the default period for presentation is no later than 21 calendar days after shipment. This presentation must, however, be made no later than the expiry date of the documentary credit. The individual transport articles each contain rules as to what is considered to be the shipment date for the specific document. It is important to note that the sub-article applies only to an original transport document. A presentation which only includes a copy of a transport document would not be subject to this rule. Sub-article (c) is the equivalent of UCP 500 sub-article 43 (a) and includes ISBP, ICC Publication No. 645, paragraph 16. It would be advisable for the applicant in its documentary credit application, or the issuing bank in the issuance of the documentary credit, to provide an indication of the number of days following the date of shipment within which presentation is to be made rather than relying on a default period that may not meet the requirements of the underlying transaction.

Sub-article (d) is the equivalent of the second sentence of UCP 500 article 21 and the last sentence of the first paragraph of UCP 500 sub-article 13 (a). The essential concept contained in UCP 500 that data be not inconsistent with any other stipulated document has been changed to reflect that the data in a document, when read in context with the documentary credit, the document itself and international standard banking practice, does not need to be identical, but must not conflict with data in the same document, any other stipulated document or the documentary credit. During the drafting process, the Drafting Group questioned ICC national committees as to the need to review data in a document as against data in any other stipulated document. The overwhelming response from national committees was to retain this principle in document examination.

Over the years, the approach by banks to documents that may be deemed to be inconsistent with one another has been proved, in many cases, to be subject to misuse due to a misinterpretation of the rule. When inconsistencies encompassed issues including simple typing and grammatical errors, banks frequently cited a significant number of discrepancies. However, calling many of these discrepancies was often unwarranted. The Drafting Group believed that this concept needed to be changed and felt that the phrase specifying that data must not "conflict with" would be a much narrower and more preferable concept than one stating "documents which appear on their face to be inconsistent with" and would require banks to make a decision based on the compliance of the data itself. The Drafting Group believes this will result in a reduction of discrepancies. Consequently, this new standard does not require a mirror image of data.

Sub-article (d) also refers to "when read in context" as an additional qualification of "not in conflict". A number of questions arose during the course of the revision as to the meaning and application of "not in conflict". The requirements of the documentary credit, the structure and purpose of the document itself and international standard banking practice need to be assessed, understood and be taken into consideration in determining compliance of a document. For example, data concerning the consignee in a certificate of origin that differs from the consignee data in the bill of lading would not be considered as being in conflict. The consignee may well be a bank that takes an interest in the goods as a security for its financing or is indicated as consignee to prevent the applicant from claiming the goods without presentation of an original bill of lading. The consignee stated in the certificate of origin is there for customs purposes, whereas the consignee in the bill of lading refers to the function of the document as a document of title. Both parties are named "consignee" but serve different purposes for different addressees in the documents.

In addition, the new standard of "not conflict with" relates the data contained in the document to what was required by the documentary credit, to what is stated in any other stipulated document and to international standard banking practice. International standard banking practice, some of which is contained in the ISBP, ICC Publication No. 681, goes beyond the practices contained in this publication and also includes additional practices of the industry that have become standard. These may include practices carried out by document checkers on a daily basis that are not articulated in this publication. In addition, it must be recognized that the ISBP does not cover every type of document called for under a documentary credit.

Sub-article 14 (e) is the equivalent of the second sentence of UCP 500 sub-article 37 (c). It has been moved to this article to be in line with the new structure introducing one article to describe the standard for examination of documents, including the requirements that apply to all or a number of documents. The sub-article specifically addresses the fact that the description of goods, services or performances in documents other than the commercial invoice may be in general terms as long as it does not conflict with the description contained in the documentary credit. By using the words "if stated", it also emphasizes that there is no need for a goods description to appear on every document. This is a clear reference to those ICC national committees that, during the revision process, believed that the UCP should include reference to linkage in the documents, which included having a goods description on each document presented as one of the ways to achieve "linkage". UCP 600 does not refer to, require or imply that linkage is necessary between or among documents.

The first sentence of UCP 500 article 21 is now part of UCP 600 sub-article 14 (f). It contains the additional stipulation that a document must appear to fulfil the function of the document required by the documentary credit and otherwise comply with UCP 600 sub-article 14 (d) regarding conflicting data. This requirement means that it must be determinable that the document fulfils the intent required. This does not mean, however, that a document checker must have knowledge of all of the specific requirements for the document, but rather that he must be able to recognize that its intended purpose is that required in the documentary credit. For example, a weight list that does not offer any information as to the weight obviously would not appear to fulfil the function of a weight list. Similarly, a document that purports to be a certificate of analysis that does not contain any data regarding analysis or reference to the goods being analyzed would not appear to fulfil the function of a certificate of analysis.

It should be remembered that the application of the rule regarding a document fulfilling its function is not limited to the situation in which the documentary credit calls for a document other than transport documents, insurance documents or commercial invoices without specifying its required content. It emphasizes that an issuing bank has a responsibility to ensure that the documentary credit contains sufficient requirements, in a clear and unambiguous manner, for the documents requested. If an applicant requests a document as simple as a "packing list" without further description, it must have some expectations as to the content of that document. The beneficiary need not elaborate on the required content; it may present a packing list in any form that fulfils the function of a packing list.

UCP 500 sub-article 13 (a) provided that a document not required under the documentary credit may be returned to the presenter or passed on without responsibility. Sub-article (g) provides a modified equivalent rule. The article now states that in this case the document will be disregarded by banks and may be returned to the presenter. Under UCP 500, banks would return additional documents to a beneficiary and were caught up in unnecessary correspondence as to why that course of action was taken when the UCP allowed banks to forward without responsibility.

Sub-article (h) remains the same as it was in UCP 500 sub-article 13 (c). Soon after the introduction of UCP 500, ICC issued Position Paper No. 3, which unfortunately introduced new issues, further confusing practitioners' understanding of UCP 500 sub-article 13 (c). During the course of the revision, the Drafting Group proposed several alternatives to ICC national committees for the treatment of non-documentary conditions, aimed at a wording different from that in UCP 500 which would allow for a different interpretation and application; however, none of these was considered to be preferable to the existing rule. Whilst the language in UCP 600 is basically the same as that in UCP 500, the interpretation of sub-article 14 (h) should be narrower than that offered by Position Paper No. 3, which referred to UCP 500 sub-article 13 (c) concerning non-documentary conditions and a concept of "linkage". The position under UCP 600 is that if a documentary credit stipulates a condition without indicating the document required for compliance, the bank should simply treat the condition as if it did not exist and disregard it. The data in documents will still be subject to review under sub-article 14 (d) to ensure that any data is not conflicting. The issues covered by sub-article (h) can be easily resolved by issuing banks' and applicants' ensuring that any term or condition, stated in the documentary credit is clearly linked to a stipulated document. For example, instead of "Shipment by conference line vessel" the documentary credit may state, "Shipping company certificate stating the goods are shipped on a conference line vessel" or "Bill of lading to indicate shipment by conference line vessel".

Sub-article (i) creates a simple rule stating that a document may be dated prior to the issuance date of the documentary credit; however, the document must not be dated later than the date it is presented to the bank. This rule is similar to that contained in UCP 500 article 22 and seeks to overcome situations in which banks often needlessly refused documents because they were dated after the date of shipment. For example, it is not unusual for an inspection certificate to be dated after the date of shipment. In itself, this does not imply that the goods inspected were different from those that were shipped. It merely indicates the dating of the document. Clearly, if a document is dated after the date of shipment and states "we have today inspected" or similar, the implication is that different goods were inspected, and the document would be discrepant.

Under UCP 500, discrepancies in documents were often based on the differences in the addresses of the applicant and the beneficiary from those stated in the documentary credit. In practice, however, companies often have many different offices (sales offices, warehouses, shipping departments, etc.) involved in the export or import of goods or services. Sub-article (j) states that, where shown in documents, these addresses need not be the same as those stated in the documentary credit provided that they are in the same country as the respective addresses contained in the documentary credit. The sub-article goes further to state that additional contact details as part of the beneficiary's or applicant's addresses will be disregarded, a position that was reflected in ISBP, ICC Publication No. 645, paragraphs 60 and 61. In the sub-article, however, there is an exception to this rule: when the address or contact details of the applicant appear as part of the consignee or notify party on a transport document, the rule does not apply. In this case, the address and contact details (if any) must be the same as those stated in the documentary credit.

UCP 600 sub-article 14 (k) widens the scope of the rule provided in UCP 500 sub-article 31 (iii). Not only does the shipper or consignor on a transport document not have to be the beneficiary of the documentary credit, which was the case under UCP 500, but also the shipper or consignor on any document required by the documentary credit need not be the beneficiary.

Lastly, sub-article (l) provides that a transport document may be issued by any party other than the carrier, owner, master or charterer provided it meets the requirements for transport documents in UCP 600 articles 19, 20, 21, 22, 23 or 24. This is an exception to the general approach in UCP 600 not to have repetition of requirements. Whilst reviewing the need for rules that existed in UCP 500, the Drafting Group came to the conclusion that UCP 500 article 30 was not necessary. This article, covering transport documents issued by freight forwarders, required such a transport document to be signed or otherwise authenticated by the freight forwarder as carrier or multimodal transport operator or be signed or otherwise authenticated as a named agent for or on behalf of the carrier or multimodal transport operator. When compared to the applicable transport articles of UCP 500 (articles 23–28), the Drafting Group could draw no distinction between these articles and article 30. The transport articles did not refer to those documents being "issued" by the carrier or other party.

In earlier drafts of this article, no equivalent of sub-article (l) was included. Following extensive communication between representatives of the ICC Transport Commission and the Drafting Group, it was pointed out that the transport industry had concerns that having no equivalent of UCP 500 article 30 could lead banks to refuse documents issued by freight forwarders (despite being signed by them as carrier or as a named agent for or on behalf of the carrier). Whilst the Drafting Group did not share these concerns, it was finally agreed to include the content of sub-article (l), which broadens the concept contained in UCP 500 to cover any party, which includes freight forwarders among others. The only requirement for the issuer of the transport document is that it must fulfil the requirements found in the respective transport document articles of UCP 600.

Cross-references within UCP 600

- Article 2 – definitions of "Complying presentation" and "Presenter";
- Article 12 on nomination;
- Sub-article 16 (d) on notice of refusal;
- Article 18 on commercial invoices;
- Articles 19–25 on transport documents;
- Article 29 on extension of the period for presentation;
- Article 35 concerning documents lost in transit.

Article 15

Complying Presentation

a. When an issuing bank determines that a presentation is complying, it must honour.

b. When a confirming bank determines that a presentation is complying, it must honour or negotiate and forward the documents to the issuing bank.

c. When a nominated bank determines that a presentation is complying and honours or negotiates, it must forward the documents to the confirming bank or issuing bank.

Changes from UCP 500

- New article to reflect the action required when a complying presentation is made;
- New rule concerning when an issuing bank honours;
- New rule concerning when a confirming bank honours or negotiates;
- New rule concerning when a nominated bank acting on its nomination honours or negotiates;
- New rules concerning the confirming and nominated banks' forwarding of documents.

Commentary

Article 15 is a new article in UCP 600, which specifically states at what point honour or negotiation takes place when a complying presentation has been made. The article is broken down into three sub-articles that deal separately with the issuing bank, the confirming bank and a nominated bank.

Sub-article (a) addresses the issuing bank's obligation to honour when it has determined that a presentation is complying. An issuing bank honours without regard to whether it has been reimbursed by the applicant.

Sub-article (b) addresses a confirming bank's obligation to honour or negotiate and forward the documents to the issuing bank when it has determined that a presentation is complying.

Sub-article (c) addresses a nominated bank's obligation. This obligation is subject to the extent to which a nominated bank has agreed to act in accordance with its nomination, as expressed in a separate communication to the beneficiary. When it has determined that a presentation is complying and honours or negotiates, it has an obligation to forward the documents to the confirming bank or issuing bank.

The essential word in each of the sub-articles is "when". The introduction of this concept was necessary as a result of the removal from the UCP of the term "reasonable time" in relation to examination of documents and the provision in article 14 of a maximum of five banking days following the day of presentation to determine compliance.

The word "when" does not mean immediately, but indicates that the process of honour or negotiation must begin. During the normal workflow for documentary credits, it can often take some time after the actual determination that the documents comply to conclude the processing of the transaction. This could range from an hour to a day, depending on the work flow and the time of day that the determination is made. Banks regularly have cut-off times for the processing of work late in the day, which can mean that an actual payment might not be effected until the following day.

The reference to the forwarding of documents was seen as a critical issue for a number of ICC national committees, who commented that nominated banks did not release the documents immediately, even in cases where the nominated bank had been reimbursed.

Cross-references within UCP 600

- Article 2 – definitions of "Complying presentation", "Confirming bank", "Honour", "Issuing bank", "Negotiation" and "Nominated bank";
- Article 7 on issuing bank's undertaking;
- Article 8 on confirming bank's undertaking;
- Article 12 on nomination.

ARTICLE 16

Discrepant Documents, Waiver and Notice

a. When a nominated bank acting on its nomination, a confirming bank, if any, or the issuing bank determines that a presentation does not comply, it may refuse to honour or negotiate.

b. When an issuing bank determines that a presentation does not comply, it may in its sole judgement approach the applicant for a waiver of the discrepancies. This does not, however, extend the period mentioned in sub-article 14 (b).

c. When a nominated bank acting on its nomination, a confirming bank, if any, or the issuing bank decides to refuse to honour or negotiate, it must give a single notice to that effect to the presenter.

The notice must state:

i. that the bank is refusing to honour or negotiate; and

ii. each discrepancy in respect of which the bank refuses to honour or negotiate; and

iii. a) that the bank is holding the documents pending further instructions from the presenter; or

b) that the issuing bank is holding the documents until it receives a waiver from the applicant and agrees to accept it, or receives further instructions from the presenter prior to agreeing to accept a waiver; or

c) that the bank is returning the documents; or

d) that the bank is acting in accordance with instructions previously received from the presenter.

d. The notice required in sub-article 16 (c) must be given by telecommunication or, if that is not possible, by other expeditious means no later than the close of the fifth banking day following the day of presentation.

e. A nominated bank acting on its nomination, a confirming bank, if any, or the issuing bank may, after providing notice required by sub-article 16 (c) (iii) (a) or (b), return the documents to the presenter at any time.

f. If an issuing bank or a confirming bank fails to act in accordance with the provisions of this article, it shall be precluded from claiming that the documents do not constitute a complying presentation.

g. When an issuing bank refuses to honour or a confirming bank refuses to honour or negotiate and has given notice to that effect in accordance with this article, it shall then be entitled to claim a refund, with interest, of any reimbursement made.

Changes from UCP 500

- Addition of two new alternatives for the handling of a presentation that does not comply;
- Notice of refusal to honour or negotiate to be given no later than the fifth banking day following the day of presentation;
- Return of the documents to a presenter at any time after having given notice that documents are held by a confirming or issuing bank pending instructions from the presenter;
- Honour or negotiation under reserve or indemnity is no longer covered in UCP 600.

Commentary

During the life of UCP 500, article 14 was one of the articles prompting the most queries to the ICC Banking Commission. As a result, in 2002 ICC issued a paper entitled "Examination of Documents, Waiver of Discrepancies and notice under UCP 500". This document enhanced the understanding of UCP 500 article 14 and, as a result, was used by the Drafting Group to revise UCP 500 article 14. The equivalent UCP 600 article is article 16.

Whilst UCP 600 article 15 explains the obligations and process in relation to compliant presentations, sub-article (a) starts with the basic rule related to the processing of documents that do not comply by simply stating that a nominated bank acting on its nomination, a confirming bank, if any, or the issuing bank may refuse to honour or negotiate such a presentation.

Sub-article (b) follows with a rule allowing the issuing bank to approach the applicant for a waiver of discrepancies. The rule only applies to the issuing bank, because it is the only bank having a direct relationship with the applicant of the credit. While this sub-article allows the issuing bank to approach the applicant, this is at the discretion of the issuing bank. A request from a beneficiary, confirming bank or nominated bank for the issuing bank to approach the applicant for a waiver does not place an obligation on the issuing bank to do so. There is no rule in the UCP that requires the issuing bank to seek a waiver of the discrepancies from the applicant. Even if the issuing bank approaches the applicant for a waiver, this does not extend the maximum of five banking days following the day of presentation for giving notice to the presenter.

Sub-article (c) details the specific steps to be taken by a nominated bank acting on its nomination, a confirming bank or an issuing bank when providing a notice of refusal. As stated in the article, the notice must be a single notice to the presenter. The bank may not give multiple notices in relation to the same presentation.

Sub-articles (c) (i) (ii) and (iii) concern the specific information to be provided with the notice. In accordance with (c) (i), the notice must first state that the bank is refusing to honour or negotiate. Sub-article (c) (ii) says that the notice must also indicate each discrepancy that is the basis for the refusal. Note that the sub-article states "each discrepancy". It is not sufficient to list one discrepancy or to give a partial list if more than one discrepancy is found. The list must be complete and be specific as to the reason each is considered to be a discrepancy. Discrepancies such as "invoice not as per LC" or "conflicting data between documents" would not be considered to be specific reasons for refusal.

Sub-article (c) (iii) lists four options, one of which must be contained in a bank's notice of refusal. UCP 500 provided only two options in sub-article 14 (d) (ii) – to return the documents or to hold them at the disposal of the presenter. Two of the options contained in UCP 600 sub-articles (c) (iii) (a) and (c) are that the bank can say it is either holding the documents pending further instructions from the presenter or is returning the documents. Note that the requirement to state that the bank is holding documents "at the disposal of the presenter" is no longer contained in the UCP.

The two new options are (iii) (b) and (d). Sub-article (c) (iii) (b) states that the issuing bank is holding documents until it receives a waiver from the applicant and agrees to accept it, or receives further instructions from the presenter prior to agreeing to accept a waiver from the applicant. As stated in sub-article (b), the issuing bank may seek a waiver from the applicant; however, it has no obligation to do so. Likewise, if it does, it has no obligation to accept a waiver it receives from the applicant. It is sometimes the case that the issuing bank will receive instructions from the presenter to handle the documents differently prior to receiving a waiver of discrepancies. Should this be the case, this sub-article gives the option for the issuing bank to handle the document in the manner instructed by the presenter, based on whether the waiver or the instructions are received first. The wording contained in sub-article (c) (iii) (b) will not be new to a large number of documentary credit practitioners. This wording, or wording of a similar nature, was used in a considerable number of notices of refusal given under UCP 500. The problem was that the wording did not reflect the options that were available under UCP 500 sub-article 14 (d) (ii), i.e., that the documents are being held at the disposal of, or being returned to, the presenter. In reality, the wording that was incorporated into those notices of refusal reflected the practice of banks as opposed to the requirements of UCP 500 sub-article 14 (d) (ii). That practice has now been recognized and incorporated as one of the options available under sub-article (c) (iii).

Sub-article (c) (iii) (d) addresses the situation in which, as part of the presentation of the document, the presenter may, if there are discrepancies, give instructions for handling the documents. In this case the notice, in addition to stating that the bank is refusing to honour or negotiate and listing the specific discrepancies, may simply state that the bank is acting in accordance with the instructions previously received.

Sub-article (d) states that the notice required in sub-article (c) must be given by telecommunication or other expeditious means no later than the close of the fifth banking day following the day of presentation. This reflects the reduced time period for giving notice of acceptance or refusal in sub-article 14 (b).

When handling discrepant documents, it is often the case that the refusal notice is provided and instructions are sought from the presenter or a waiver is requested, but no response is received. Sub-article (e) gives a bank (a nominated bank acting on its nomination, a confirming bank, if any, or the issuing bank) the option of simply returning the documents to the presenter. Of course, this sub-article is subject to the bank having previously provided the notice required by sub-article (c) (iii) (a) or (b), as stated in the rule. The expectation, although not obligatory, is that banks will give prior notice of the date they will return the documents rather than taking arbitrary action.

Sub-article (f) is the equivalent of UCP 500 sub-article 14 (e), which says that the issuing or confirming bank is precluded from claiming that the presentation is non-complying if it fails to act in accordance with the article.

Sub-article (g) is the equivalent of UCP 500 sub-article 14 (d) (iii). When an issuing bank or confirming bank has provided a reimbursement instruction to a nominated bank and that nominated bank has reimbursed itself and, when the issuing bank has subsequently provided a refusal notice according to article 16, the issuing bank will be entitled to claim a refund of the reimbursement made plus interest, from the time the account of the issuing bank has been debited until the date refund is made.

UCP 500 sub-article 14 (f) relating to negotiation under a reserve or indemnity has not been incorporated into UCP 600. The Drafting Group felt that this sub-article dealt with a situation subject to an agreement between a nominated bank and the beneficiary and was not an essential part of the UCP.

Cross-references within UCP 600

- Article 2 – Definitions of "Applicant", "Banking Day", "Complying presentation", "Confirming bank", "Honour", "Issuing bank", Negotiation", "Presentation" and "Presenter";
- Article 7, on issuing bank undertaking;
- Article 8 on confirming bank undertaking;
- Article 12 – Nomination – on liability of a nominated bank.

Article 17

Original Documents and Copies

a. At least one original of each document stipulated in the credit must be presented.

b. A bank shall treat as an original any document bearing an apparently original signature, mark, stamp, or label of the issuer of the document, unless the document itself indicates that it is not an original.

c. Unless a document indicates otherwise, a bank will also accept a document as original if it:

   i. appears to be written, typed, perforated or stamped by the document issuer's hand; or

   ii. appears to be on the document issuer's original stationery; or

   iii. states that it is original, unless the statement appears not to apply to the document presented.

d. If a credit requires presentation of copies of documents, presentation of either originals or copies is permitted.

e. If a credit requires presentation of multiple documents by using terms such as "in duplicate", "in two fold" or "in two copies", this will be satisfied by the presentation of at least one original and the remaining number in copies, except when the document itself indicates otherwise.

Changes from UCP 500

- Need to present one original of each document stipulated in the credit (refers to ISBP, ICC Publication No. 645, paragraph 32);
- Presentation of originals in lieu of copies acceptable (refers to ISBP, ICC Publication No. 645, paragraph 34).

Commentary

In the late 1990s, a number of queries to the ICC Banking Commission and several court cases raised the issue of what constitutes an original document under UCP 500 sub-article 20 (b). These issues prompted the ICC Banking Commission in July 1999 to issue a Decision on "The determination of an 'Original' document in the context of UCP 500 sub-Article 20(b)". Since that time, no further requests for Opinions as to what constitutes an "original" document have been received by ICC.

As a result of the issuance and acceptance of the Decision on originals, the UCP Drafting Group decided to use the Decision as the basis for the revision of UCP 500 sub-article 20 (b). UCP 600 sub-articles 17 (b) and (c) reflect the incorporation of the essential positions of the Decision into UCP 600. Although written under UCP 500, the Decision remains valid under UCP 600. The Appendix to the revised ISBP (ICC Publication No. 681), which brings the ISBP into line with UCP 600, includes the Decision as further guidance on originals and copies.

Article 17 incorporates the general principles contained in UCP 500 sub-articles 20 (b) and (c).

Sub-article (a) sets the general rule regarding the presentation of documents and states the position that at least one original of each document stipulated in the credit must be presented.

Sub-article (d) makes it clear that the request for a presentation of copies can be satisfied by the presentation of either originals or copies. Copies would include photocopies. Copies of documents need not be signed. The position regarding copies not requiring a signature is also covered in ISBP, ICC Publication No. 681, paragraph 32.

Following the logic of sub-article (a), sub-article (e) refers to and maintains the principle of UCP 500 sub-article 20 (c) (ii), that when the credit calls for the presentation of multiple documents (in duplicate, two-fold, etc.), at least one original must be presented. Credits should be precise in their wording concerning the number of originals and copies required to be presented. If originals and copies are required, the credit must be specific as to the number of originals and the number of copies required. If the intention is to only require copies of documents, then the credit must be precise in its requirement for copies.

Cross-references within UCP 600

- Article 2 – Definition of "Credit";
- Article 3 – Interpretations.

ARTICLE 18

Commercial Invoice

a. A commercial invoice:

   i. must appear to have been issued by the beneficiary (except as provided in article 38);

   ii. must be made out in the name of the applicant (except as provided in sub-article 38 (g));

   iii. must be made out in the same currency as the credit; and

   iv. need not be signed.

b. A nominated bank acting on its nomination, a confirming bank, if any, or the issuing bank may accept a commercial invoice issued for an amount in excess of the amount permitted by the credit, and its decision will be binding upon all parties, provided the bank in question has not honoured or negotiated for an amount in excess of that permitted by the credit.

c. The description of the goods, services or performance in a commercial invoice must correspond with that appearing in the credit.

CHANGES FROM UCP 500

- The invoice must be made out in the same currency as the credit (refers to ISBP, ICC Publication No. 645, paragraph 64);
- Emphasis on the acceptability of a commercial invoice issued for a greater amount than the credit;
- Change to add the description of "services" or "performance" in addition to the former wording only mentioning "goods";
- Removal of the second sentence of UCP 500 sub-article 37 (c) ("In all other documents, the goods may be described in general terms not inconsistent with the description of the goods in the Credit") and moving it to sub-article 14 (e).

Commentary

Sub-article (a) (iii) has a new requirement that the invoice must be made out in the same currency as the credit, reflecting the value of the goods, services or performance. In some countries, due to their exchange control requirements, the invoice may have to show a local currency equivalent. If the invoice is made out in a local currency showing an equivalent amount in the currency of the credit, the invoice will be deemed to be discrepant. However, it will be acceptable if the invoice is made out in the same currency as the credit and also shows a local currency equivalent.

Sub-article (b) reflects a change to describe the acceptability by a nominated bank, a confirming bank, if any, or the issuing bank of a commercial invoice issued for an amount in excess of the amount permitted by the documentary credit, provided banks do not honour or negotiate for an amount in excess of the amount permitted by the documentary credit. UCP 500 sub-article 37 (b) began with a negative statement, saying that unless otherwise stipulated in the credit, banks "may refuse" commercial invoices issued for amounts in excess of the amount permitted by the credit. This UCP 500 wording was considered to implicitly encourage a refusal of documents, whereas in UCP 600 the emphasis is on acceptance, supporting the fundamental idea that the UCP are rules for payment.

The change in the wording of sub-article (c) includes a reference to "services" or "performance", reflecting the position that documentary credits do not only cover the shipment of goods. Similar to the provision in UCP 500 sub-article 37 (c), commercial invoices are required to contain a description of the goods, services or performance that corresponds with the description in the credit. Applying the standard of "correspond with" in this instance has now become established under international standard banking practice. Therefore, the Drafting Group saw no reason to change the current interpretation or construction of this sub-article.

Cross-references within UCP 600

- Article 2 – Definitions of "Applicant", "Beneficiary", "Nominated bank", "Confirming bank", "Issuing bank" and "Credit";
- Sub-article 14 (e) – Standard for Examination of Documents – description of goods on documents other than commercial invoices.

ARTICLE 19

Transport Document Covering at Least Two Different Modes of Transport

a. A transport document covering at least two different modes of transport (multimodal or combined transport document), however named, must appear to:

i. indicate the name of the carrier and be signed by:

- the carrier or a named agent for or on behalf of the carrier, or
- the master or a named agent for or on behalf of the master.

Any signature by the carrier, master or agent must be identified as that of the carrier, master or agent.

Any signature by an agent must indicate whether the agent has signed for or on behalf of the carrier or for or on behalf of the master.

ii. indicate that the goods have been dispatched, taken in charge or shipped on board at the place stated in the credit, by:

- pre-printed wording, or
- a stamp or notation indicating the date on which the goods have been dispatched, taken in charge or shipped on board.

The date of issuance of the transport document will be deemed to be the date of dispatch, taking in charge or shipped on board, and the date of shipment. However, if the transport document indicates, by stamp or notation, a date of dispatch, taking in charge or shipped on board, this date will be deemed to be the date of shipment.

iii. indicate the place of dispatch, taking in charge or shipment and the place of final destination stated in the credit, even if:

a) the transport document states, in addition, a different place of dispatch, taking in charge or shipment or place of final destination, or

b) the transport document contains the indication "intended" or similar qualification in relation to the vessel, port of loading or port of discharge.

iv. be the sole original transport document or, if issued in more than one original, be the full set as indicated on the transport document.

v. contain terms and conditions of carriage or make reference to another source containing the terms and conditions of carriage (short form or blank back transport document). Contents of terms and conditions of carriage will not be examined.

vi. contain no indication that it is subject to a charter party.

b. For the purpose of this article, transhipment means unloading from one means of conveyance and reloading to another means of conveyance (whether or not in different modes of transport) during the carriage from the place of dispatch, taking in charge or shipment to the place of final destination stated in the credit.

c. i. A transport document may indicate that the goods will or may be transhipped provided that the entire carriage is covered by one and the same transport document.

ii. A transport document indicating that transhipment will or may take place is acceptable, even if the credit prohibits transhipment.

Changes from UCP 500

- Rearrangement of articles so that the present article precedes articles dealing with the marine/ocean bill of lading, non-negotiable sea waybill and charter party bill of lading;
- Title of the article refers, not to a name of a document, but to the way the transportation takes place;
- Deletion of "multimodal transport" in the title;
- Deletion of reference to "multimodal transport operator";
- Rewording of the term "Multimodal Transport Document";
- Deletion of "If a Credit calls for", "banks will, unless otherwise stipulated in the Credit, accept a document";
- Deletion of reference to "appears on its face", as this is now referred to solely in sub-article 14 (a) as a general principle covering all stipulated documents;
- Deletion of "or otherwise authenticated", "authentication" and "authenticating" due to the interpretation of signing in article 3;
- Standard wording for the manner in which a transport document is to indicate the name of the carrier and that the transport document must be prepared in such a way that it is possible to identify in which capacity the party signing the document does sign – as carrier, master or agent;
- No requirement for the name of the master where an agent signs;
- Wording to make it clear that the transport document must evidence that the goods have been dispatched, taken in charge or shipped on board at the place stated in the documentary credit;
- Wording to make it clear that the transport document must evidence transportation between the places stated in the documentary credit;
- Deletion of reference to vessels propelled by sail;

- Deletion of "in all other respects meets the stipulations of the Credit". This provision is not required due to the definition of "Complying presentation" in article 2;
- Transhipment provisions have now been split across two sub-articles to accommodate a general definition for the type of transport covered by the article, the provisions applicable when transhipment is evidenced within the transport document and the effect of transhipment when the documentary credit prohibits such action.

Commentary

This article applies when the documentary credit requires presentation of a transport document covering transport by more than one mode of transport.

Because transport by more than one mode of transport is the more common form in which goods are transported from seller to buyer, the Drafting Group placed this article as the first of the transport document articles. Because more transport companies seek to control the entire carriage of a cargo from its place of origin to the place of its use, the rules reflect the increasing importance of a single document covering the entire carriage, regardless of which mode of transport or means of conveyance is involved during the journey. Likewise, beneficiaries and applicants are interested in having one single counterpart that takes care of the entire carriage rather than having to address different parties for each leg and mode or means of conveyance used.

The wording in the title is in contrast to that in the later articles referring to a bill of lading, non-negotiable sea waybill, charter party bill of lading, etc., since these documents have a traditional background and history linked to their names and are recognized by name by exporters, importers, banks, shipping companies and forwarders. A document "covering at least two different modes of transport" is a relatively new concept and still lacks specific name recognition. The rules, therefore, allow for a document, however named, that appears to cover transportation by at least two different modes of transportation.

The wording of sub-article (a) does not refer to any particular name of a document. Rather, it describes the way the goods are being moved utilizing at least two different modes of transport, for example by truck and then by vessel or rail. There have been so many different names assigned to this type of document, including "Multimodal Transport Document", "Combined Transport Bill of Lading", "Intermodal Transport Document", etc., that the Drafting Group thought it best to describe what happens during the carriage rather than to refer to the name or title of a document. Although the wording in brackets refers to a "multimodal or combined transport document", this is to indicate links with terminology used under UCP 500. The nature of the document is a more important consideration than stating a name of the transport document.

Wording to the effect that "If a Credit calls for a transport document covering at least two different modes of transport (multimodal transport), banks will, unless otherwise stipulated in the Credit, accept a document ..." was considered to be unnecessary. It was decided that the rules should only stipulate the requirements linked to the document rather than referring to what banks will accept if a credit calls for such a document. Likewise, it was considered unnecessary to repeat "unless otherwise stipulated in the credit", since this, as indicated earlier in the Commentary, is taken care of by the general stipulation "unless expressly modified or excluded by the credit" in article 1.

As is the case for all other transport documents, there is no reference to "on its face" in this article. The decision was made by the Drafting Group that there should be a reference to "on its face" or "on their face" in UCP 600, but that there was only a need for this to appear in one place, sub-article 14 (a).

The deletion of "or otherwise authenticated", "authentication" and "authenticating" in relation to the manner in which these transport documents are signed follows the principle adopted for all of the transport articles. The interpretation of signing in article 3 covers these situations by including a reference to "... any other mechanical or electronic method of authentication".

Sub-article (a) (i) requires that the name of the carrier be indicated on the transport document. This can be by a specific reference within the body of the transport document, e.g., "ABC Co. Ltd, the carrier" or by the way the respective document is signed, e.g., "For ABC Co. Ltd as carrier". The manner of signing described here is not exclusive and would include circumstances such as those in which a named agent signs for or on behalf of the [named] carrier.

It should be noted that the manner in which transport documents covered by this article indicate the name of the carrier and are to be signed has not changed between UCP 500 and UCP 600. The only exception to the signing requirements occurs when the transport document is signed by an agent for or on behalf of the master. In this event, it is not necessary to state the master's name.

As one example of indicating the capacity of the carrier, if a document is issued by a company called "XYZ SL Ltd" or "XYZ Ltd", it would be difficult to assess whether either company is a carrier. A document checker will only be able to determine that the document appears to have been issued by the company "XYZ SL Ltd" or "XYZ Ltd", but not the capacity in which the company is acting. Therefore, whatever the name of the company that issued the transport document, an indication to the effect that the issuing company or another company is the carrier is required. This requirement will also be fulfilled if the party signing the document indicates that it is signing "as carrier", or as agent for a named carrier.

To take another example, while it may appear that a transport document issued by a company called "ABC Shipping Lines Ltd" is a document that indicates the name of the carrier, unless the word "carrier" appears on the transport document linked to the name of the company, the company name in and of itself will not be sufficient.

Sub-article (a) (i) also goes on to describe what is required by way of signature. The party signing the transport document must indicate whether it is signing as carrier, master or agent, and if the party is signing as agent, the name of that agent must be included, as well as the capacity in which it is signing. Therefore, a simple signature on the transport document does not suffice. The indication of the capacity of the one signing the transport document must also appear in the signature space. However, if the transport document shows the name of the issuing company together with the indication "carrier", a simple signature in the signature box with the indication "for and on behalf of [name of the issuing company]" or "for and on behalf of the carrier" or a similar indication would be sufficient.

The rules require that an agent signing the transport document must indicate whether it is signing for or on behalf of the carrier or for or on behalf of the master. The transportation industry pointed out that it is quite common for agents not to know the name of the master of a vessel at the time the transport document is issued, and therefore the name of the master should not need to be indicated on the transport document. This has been recognized by the rules, which require that the carrier and a named agent be indicated, but has no such requirement for the master's name. It should be noted under this sub-article that the document may no longer be signed in the capacity of multimodal transport operator or by a named agent signing for or on behalf of the multimodal transport operator. In discussions with the ICC Transport Commission it was determined that in most cases it is a carrier or agent that signs this type of document; a party signing as "Multimodal Transport Operator" was seldom seen.

Sub-article (a) (ii) requires that the transport document indicate that the goods have been dispatched, taken in charge or shipped on board at the place stated in the documentary credit by pre-printed wording. The date of issuance of the transport document will be deemed to be the date of shipment. The words "at the place stated in the credit" have been specifically included to emphasize that banks must be able to determine from the transport document, not only that the goods were dispatched, taken in charge or shipped on board within the latest shipment date stated in the documentary credit, but also that there is evidence that the date of shipment relates to the dispatch, taking in charge or shipment from the place stated in the documentary credit and not from any other place of receipt or taking in charge that may be evidenced within the transport document.

Sub-article (a) (ii) also states that an indication of dispatch, taking in charge or shipped on board may be determined by a stamp or notation indicating the date on which the goods have been dispatched, taken in charge or shipped on board. When the transport document includes a stamp or notation, the date shown therein as the date of dispatch, taking in charge or shipped on board will be deemed to be the date of shipment whether or not this date is prior to or after the date of issuance of the transport document.

The transport document must appear to indicate that dispatch, taking in charge or shipment has been effected from the place stated in the documentary credit to the place of final destination stated in the documentary credit, even if the transport document shows the word "intended" in relation to the vessel, port of loading or port of discharge. Sub-article (a) (iii) refers to this.

Sub-article (a) (iii) permits the transport document to indicate other places relating to the journey of the goods prior to the place of dispatch, taking in charge or shipment, or after the place of final destination mentioned in the documentary credit. This allows a carrier to issue a document which covers, not only the journey foreseen by the documentary credit, but the entire journey of the goods. For example, under a documentary credit that requires the transport document to cover shipment from Europe to Hong Kong, a transport document showing Bern, Switzerland – which is not a city providing access to ocean going vessels – as the place of dispatch or taking in charge, Marseille as the port of loading, Hong Kong as the port of discharge and Shanghai as place of final destination would be acceptable.

Sub-article (a) (iv) continues to stress the UCP 500 position that the transport document must appear to be the sole original document that has been issued or, if it indicates that it has been issued in more than one original, all of the stated originals must be presented unless the documentary credit indicates the disposal instruction for one or more of the original transport documents.

The transport document usually contains the terms and conditions of carriage. However, as this is not always the case, sub-article (a) (v) allows for a transport document to make reference to a source other than the document itself to determine these terms and conditions. In this respect, a transport document that contains a reference to a source other than itself has generally been described as a "short form" or "blank back" transport document. Banks are not to examine the contents of the terms and conditions of carriage.

Sub-article (a) (vi) stipulates that the transport document must not contain an indication that it is subject to a charter party. The term "no indication" means that a transport document that bears any indication that it is subject to a charter party would not be acceptable under this article. As examples of "no indication", the transport document may state "to be used with charter parties" or it could contain the following data: "freight payable as per charter party" or "charter party contract number ABC123".

Since sail boats are rarely, if ever, used for transportation of goods in international trade, it was decided that a clause prohibiting presentation of a transport document indicating that the carrying vessel is propelled by sail only was no longer necessary.

Sub-article (b) provides a definition of transhipment when a transport document covering more than one mode of transport is required.

Sub-article (c) (i) explains that transhipment must be evidenced within one and the same transport document. Separate documents covering each leg of a journey would not be acceptable.

Sub-article (c) (ii) states that transhipment is allowed even when it is prohibited by the documentary credit. As transhipment always occurs when more than one mode of transport is involved, this sub-article (that was also included in UCP 500) provides a definitive rule where a documentary credit inadvertently contains a condition that transhipment is prohibited.

Cross-references in UCP 600

- Article 2 – definition of "Credit";
- Article 3 concerning interpretation of signatures;
- Article 3 concerning interpretation for determining periods of shipment;
- Sub-article 14 (c) – Standard for Examination of Documents – on the presentation period;
- Sub-article 14 (d) – Standard for Examination of Documents – on data not being in conflict;
- Sub-article 14 (e) – Standard for Examination of Documents – on goods description on documents other than the commercial invoice;
- Sub-article 14 (j) – Standard for Examination of Documents – on addresses of the applicant as consignee or notify party;
- Sub-article 14 (k) – Standard for Examination of Documents – on the shipper or consignor indicated on a document;
- Sub-article 14 (l) – Standard for Examination of Documents – on issuance of transport documents other than by the carrier or master;
- Article 17 – Original Documents and Copies;
- Article 26 – "On Deck", "Shipper's Load and Count", "Said by Shipper to Contain" and Charges Additional to Freight;
- Article 27 – Clean Transport Document;
- Article 29 – Extension of Expiry Date or Last Day for Presentation – on non-extension of latest shipment date;
- Article 31 – Partial Drawings or Shipments;
- Article 32 – Instalment Drawings or Shipments;
- Article 34 – Disclaimer on Effectiveness of Documents.

ARTICLE 20

Bill of Lading

a. A bill of lading, however named, must appear to:

i. indicate the name of the carrier and be signed by:

- the carrier or a named agent for or on behalf of the carrier, or
- the master or a named agent for or on behalf of the master.

Any signature by the carrier, master or agent must be identified as that of the carrier, master or agent.

Any signature by an agent must indicate whether the agent has signed for or on behalf of the carrier or for or on behalf of the master.

ii. indicate that the goods have been shipped on board a named vessel at the port of loading stated in the credit by:

- pre-printed wording, or
- an on board notation indicating the date on which the goods have been shipped on board.

The date of issuance of the bill of lading will be deemed to be the date of shipment unless the bill of lading contains an on board notation indicating the date of shipment, in which case the date stated in the on board notation will be deemed to be the date of shipment.

If the bill of lading contains the indication "intended vessel" or similar qualification in relation to the name of the vessel, an on board notation indicating the date of shipment and the name of the actual vessel is required.

iii. indicate shipment from the port of loading to the port of discharge stated in the credit.

If the bill of lading does not indicate the port of loading stated in the credit as the port of loading, or if it contains the indication "intended" or similar qualification in relation to the port of loading, an on board notation indicating the port of loading as stated in the credit, the date of shipment and the name of the vessel is required. This provision applies even when loading on board or shipment on a named vessel is indicated by pre-printed wording on the bill of lading.

iv. be the sole original bill of lading or, if issued in more than one original, be the full set as indicated on the bill of lading.

v. contain terms and conditions of carriage or make reference to another source containing the terms and conditions of carriage (short form or blank back bill of lading). Contents of terms and conditions of carriage will not be examined.

vi. contain no indication that it is subject to a charter party.

b. For the purpose of this article, transhipment means unloading from one vessel and reloading to another vessel during the carriage from the port of loading to the port of discharge stated in the credit.

c. i. A bill of lading may indicate that the goods will or may be transhipped provided that the entire carriage is covered by one and the same bill of lading.

ii. A bill of lading indicating that transhipment will or may take place is acceptable, even if the credit prohibits transhipment, if the goods have been shipped in a container, trailer or LASH barge as evidenced by the bill of lading.

d. Clauses in a bill of lading stating that the carrier reserves the right to tranship will be disregarded.

Changes from UCP 500

- Deletion of the words "Marine/Ocean" in the title of the article;
- Rearrangement of articles so that this article follows the one entitled "Transport Document Covering at Least Two Different Modes of Transport";
- Deletion of "If a Credit calls for", "banks will, unless otherwise stipulated in the Credit, accept a document";
- Deletion of reference to "appears on its face", as this is now referred to solely in sub-article 14 (a) as a general principle covering all stipulated documents;
- Deletion of "or otherwise authenticated", "authentication" and "authenticating" due to the interpretation of signing in article 3;
- Standard wording for the manner in which a transport document is to indicate the name of the carrier and that the transport document must be prepared in a way that it is possible to identify in which capacity the party signing the document does sign – as carrier, master or agent;
- Requirements in connection with a bill of lading showing a place of receipt or taking in charge different from the port of loading stated in the documentary credit;

- Deletion of the requirements when a bill of lading states a place of receipt or taking in charge different from the port of loading;
- Wording to make it clear that the bill of lading must evidence shipment between the port of loading and the port of discharge stated in the documentary credit;
- Deletion of reference to vessels propelled by sail;
- Deletion of "in all other respects meets the stipulations of the Credit". This provision is not required due to the definition of "Complying presentation" in article 2;
- Transhipment provisions have now been split across three sub-articles to accommodate a general definition for the type of transport covered by the article, the provisions applicable when transhipment is evidenced within the transport document, the effect of transhipment when the documentary credit prohibits such action and the allowance for clauses reserving the right to tranship.

COMMENTARY

This article applies when the documentary credit requires presentation of a bill of lading covering transport by sea from one port to another port.

During the revision process, some ICC national committees pressed for the rules to stipulate that the bill of lading must be a document of title. In that connection, issues were raised relating to clauses that began to appear on bills of lading during 2004, which suggested that carriers had the right to deliver goods covered by a bill of lading to a consignee they believed to be the rightful owner without the bill of lading being produced prior to delivery of the goods. The Drafting Group reached the conclusion that these issues could not be addressed in the UCP because it is a legal issue and the UCP are voluntary rules of contract.

Wording to the effect that "If a Credit calls for a bill of lading covering a port-to-port shipment, banks will, unless otherwise stipulated in the Credit, accept a document ..." was considered to be unnecessary. It was decided that the rules should only stipulate the requirements linked to the document rather than referring to what banks will accept if a credit calls for such a document. Likewise, it was considered unnecessary to repeat "unless otherwise stipulated in the credit", since this, as indicated earlier in the Commentary, is taken care of by the general stipulation "unless expressly modified or excluded by the credit" in article 1.

As is the case for all other transport documents, there is no reference to "on its face" in this article. The decision was made by the Drafting Group that there should be a reference to "on its face" or "on their face" in UCP 600, but that there was only a need for this to appear in one place, sub-article 14 (a).

The deletion of "or otherwise authenticated", "authentication" and "authenticating" in relation to the manner in which bills of lading are signed follows the principle adopted for all of the transport articles. The interpretation of signing in article 3 includes a reference to "... any other mechanical or electronic method of authentication".

Sub-article (a) (i) requires that the name of the carrier be indicated on the bill of lading. This can be by a specific reference to this capacity within the body of the bill of lading, e.g., "ABC Co. Ltd, the carrier" or by the way the respective document is signed, e.g., "For ABC Co. Ltd as carrier". The manner of signing described here is not exclusive and would include circumstances such as those in which a named agent signs for or on behalf of the [named] carrier.

It should be noted that the manner in which bills of lading indicate the name of the carrier and are to be signed has not changed between UCP 500 and UCP 600. The only exception to the signing requirements occurs when the bill of lading is signed by an agent for or on behalf of the master. In this event, it is not necessary to state the master's name. As explained in the Commentary to article 19, "the transportation industry pointed out it is quite common for agents not to know the name of the master of a vessel at the time the transport document is issued."

As one example of indicating the capacity of the carrier, if a document is issued by a company called "XYZ SL Ltd" or "XYZ Ltd", it would be difficult to assess whether either company is a carrier. A document checker will only be able to determine that the bill of lading appears to have been issued by the company "XYZ SL Ltd" or "XYZ Ltd", but not the capacity in which the company is acting. Therefore, whatever the name of the company that issued the bill of lading, an indication to the effect that the issuing company or another company is the carrier is required. This requirement will also be fulfilled if the party signing the bill of lading indicates that it is signing "as carrier", or as agent for a named carrier.

To take another example, while it may appear that a bill of lading issued by a company called "ABC Shipping Lines Ltd" is a bill of lading that indicates the name of the carrier, unless the word "carrier" appears on the bill of lading linked to the name of the company, the company name in and of itself will not be sufficient.

Sub-article (a) (i) also goes on to describe what is required by way of signature. The party signing the bill of lading must indicate whether it is signing as carrier, master or agent, and if the party is signing as agent, the name of that agent must be included, as well as the capacity in which it is signing. Therefore, a simple signature on the bill of lading does not suffice. The indication of the capacity of the one signing the bill of lading must also appear in the signature space. However, if the bill of lading shows the name of the issuing company together with the indication "carrier", a simple signature in the signature box with the indication "for and on behalf of [name of the issuing company]" or "for and on behalf of the carrier" or a similar indication would be sufficient.

The rules require that an agent signing the bill of lading must indicate whether it is signing for or on behalf of the carrier or for or on behalf of the master. As mentioned above, the transportation industry pointed out that it is quite common for agents not to know the name of the master of a vessel at the time a bill of lading is issued, and therefore the name of the master should not need to be indicated on the bill of lading. This has been recognized by the rules, which require that the carrier and a named agent be indicated, but has no such requirement for the master's name.

During the revision process, a number of communications were sent between the Drafting Group and representatives of the ICC Transport Commission. As a result it was agreed that the bill of lading is a transport document covering shipment from a port of loading to a port of discharge and that the rules should reflect that position. As a bill of lading covers shipment from a port to a port, the wording that appeared in UCP 500 sub-article 23 (a) (ii) was seen to encourage the presentation of a document that covered pre-carriage of the goods to the port of loading. The wording of this sub-article reads: "If the bill of lading indicates a place of receipt or taking in charge different from the port of loading, the on board notation must also include the port of loading stipulated in the Credit and the name of the vessel on which the goods have been loaded, even if they have been loaded on the vessel named in the bill of lading. This provision also applies whenever loading on board the vessel is indicated by pre-printed wording on the bill of lading."

Where pre-carriage by road, rail or air and shipment by sea is envisaged, the parties should ensure that the credit allows for a transport document to be presented that would be subject to examination under UCP 600 article 19.

The Drafting Group recognized that whilst UCP 600 conveys that the bill of lading is a port-to-port document, there will be occasions when the shipping company or its agent will include reference to a place of receipt or taking in charge that is different from the port of loading. To cover this eventuality, the content of sub-article 20 (a) (ii) reads: "indicate that the goods have been shipped on board a named vessel at the port of loading stated in the credit by: ". The emphasis in this condition is that the document checker must be able to determine that the bill of lading appears to indicate that the shipped on board statement (pre-printed wording or by a separate notation) relates to loading on board the named vessel at the port of loading stated in the credit and not to any pre-carriage of the goods between a place of receipt or taking in charge and the port of loading. Unless it is evident from the bill of lading that the shipped on board statement applies to the vessel and the port of loading, the bill of lading will require, as was the case in UCP 500, an on board notation showing the port of loading and the name of the vessel, even if the goods are loaded on the vessel named in the bill of lading. A shipped on board date will be considered to be the date of shipment. When the bill of lading includes an on board notation, the date of the on board notation will be deemed to be the date of shipment whether or not this date is prior to or after the date of issuance of the bill of lading.

When a place of receipt or taking in charge is the same as the port of loading e.g., place of receipt Hong Kong CY and port of loading Hong Kong, the conclusion given in ICC Opinion R.282 applies, namely, "Using your example where a place of receipt is given as 'Hong Kong CY' and the port of loading is shown as 'Hong Kong', they are to be deemed one and the same place and therefore not subject to the provisions of [UCP 500] sub-Article 23(a)(ii)". This opinion will also apply in respect of sub-article 20 (a) (ii).

The bill of lading must appear to indicate that shipment has been effected from the port of loading to the port of discharge as stated in the documentary credit. Sub-article (a) (iii) refers to this.

Sub-article (a) (iii) states that if a bill of lading does not indicate the port of loading stated in the documentary credit as the port of loading, it must contain an on board notation which indicates the port of loading stated in the documentary credit, the date of shipment and the name of the vessel. The same criteria apply if the bill of lading indicates the qualification "intended" or similar in respect of the port of loading.

An example of where a bill of lading does not indicate the port of loading stated in the documentary credit as the port of loading would be when the port of loading stated in the documentary credit is shown as the place of receipt, since in the field "port of loading" it shows the port where transhipment is to occur. The documentary credit requires shipment from Rotterdam to Hong Kong. Sub-article (a) (iii) requires the bill of lading to indicate shipment from the port of loading to the port of discharge stated in the credit.

The bill of lading shows:

Pre-carriage	Moon Lagoon
Place of receipt	Rotterdam
Ocean Vessel	Sun Lagoon
Port of Loading	Dubai
Port of Discharge	Hong Kong

The bill of lading will require, according to sub-article (a) (iii), an on board notation showing the vessel Moon Lagoon, the port of loading Rotterdam and the on board date.

The above example is a common structure of a bill of lading today. The shipping company or its agent seek to describe the entire journey of the goods and, as a result, the data does not appear in corresponding boxes on the bill of lading. The example is showing shipment from Rotterdam to Hong Kong with transhipment in Dubai.

A bill of lading evidencing a place of final destination different from the port of discharge as stated in the documentary credit would be acceptable.

Sub-article (a) (iv) continues to stress the UCP 500 position that the bill of lading must appear to be the sole original bill of lading that has been issued or, if it indicates that it has been issued in more than one original, all of the stated originals must be presented unless the documentary credit indicates the disposal instruction for one or more of the original bills of lading.

The bill of lading usually contains the terms and conditions of carriage. However, as this is not always the case, sub-article (a) (v) allows for a bill of lading to make reference to a source other than the document itself to determine these terms and conditions. In this respect, a bill of lading that contains a reference to a source other than itself has generally been described as a "short form" or "blank back" bill of lading. Banks are not to examine the contents of the terms and conditions of carriage.

Sub-article (a) (vi) stipulates that the bill of lading must not contain an indication that it is subject to a charter party. The term "no indication" means that a bill of lading that bears any indication that it is subject to a charter party would not be acceptable under this article. As examples of "no indication", the bill of lading may state "to be used with charter parties" or it could contain the following data: "freight payable as per charter party" or "charter party contract number ABC123".

Since sail boats are rarely, if ever, used for transportation of goods in international trade, it was decided that a clause prohibiting presentation of a bill of lading indicating that the carrying vessel is propelled by sail only was no longer necessary.

Sub-article (b) provides a definition of transhipment when a bill of lading is required.

Sub-article (c) (i) explains that transhipment must be evidenced within one and the same bill of lading. Separate documents covering each leg of a journey would not be acceptable.

Sub-article (c) (ii) recognizes the shipping industry practice that transhipment often occurs when goods are shipped in containers, trailers or LASH barges by stating that this is allowed even if prohibited by the documentary credit. The only way that an applicant can completely prohibit transhipment would be to state that transhipment is prohibited *and* that sub-article 20 (c) (ii) is not applicable or is excluded.

Sub-article (d) recognizes that a statement on a bill of lading indicating that the carrier reserves the right to do something, in this case tranship, does not imply that it has or will do so and is an acceptable condition.

Cross-references within UCP 600

- Article 2 – definition of "Credit";
- Article 3 concerning interpretation of signatures;
- Article 3 concerning interpretation for determining periods of shipment;
- Sub-article 14 (c) – Standard for Examination of Documents – on the presentation period;
- Sub-article 14 (d) – Standard for Examination of Documents – on data not being in conflict;
- Sub-article 14 (e) – Standard for Examination of Documents – on goods description on documents other than the commercial invoice;
- Sub-article 14 (j) – Standard for Examination of Documents – on addresses of the applicant as consignee or notify party;
- Sub-article 14 (k) – Standard for Examination of Documents – on shipper or consignor indicated on a document;
- Sub-article 14 (l) – Standard for Examination of Documents – on issuance of transport documents other than by the carrier, master, owner or charterer;
- Article 17 – Original Documents and Copies;
- Article 26 – "On Deck", "Shipper's Load and Count", "Said by Shipper to Contain" and Charges Additional to Freight;
- Article 27 – Clean Transport Document;
- Article 29 – Extension of Expiry Date or Last Day for Presentation – on non-extension of latest shipment date;
- Article 31 – Partial Drawings or Shipments;
- Article 32 – Instalment Drawings or Shipments;
- Article 34 – Disclaimer on Effectiveness of Documents.

ARTICLE 21

Non-Negotiable Sea Waybill

a. A non-negotiable sea waybill, however named, must appear to:

i. indicate the name of the carrier and be signed by:

- the carrier or a named agent for or on behalf of the carrier, or
- the master or a named agent for or on behalf of the master.

Any signature by the carrier, master or agent must be identified as that of the carrier, master or agent.

Any signature by an agent must indicate whether the agent has signed for or on behalf of the carrier or for or on behalf of the master.

ii. indicate that the goods have been shipped on board a named vessel at the port of loading stated in the credit by:

- pre-printed wording, or
- an on board notation indicating the date on which the goods have been shipped on board.

The date of issuance of the non-negotiable sea waybill will be deemed to be the date of shipment unless the non-negotiable sea waybill contains an on board notation indicating the date of shipment, in which case the date stated in the on board notation will be deemed to be the date of shipment.

If the non-negotiable sea waybill contains the indication "intended vessel" or similar qualification in relation to the name of the vessel, an on board notation indicating the date of shipment and the name of the actual vessel is required.

iii. indicate shipment from the port of loading to the port of discharge stated in the credit.

If the non-negotiable sea waybill does not indicate the port of loading stated in the credit as the port of loading, or if it contains the indication "intended" or similar qualification in relation to the port of loading, an on board notation indicating the port of loading as stated in the credit, the date of shipment and the name of the vessel is required. This provision applies even when loading on board or shipment on a named vessel is indicated by pre-printed wording on the non-negotiable sea waybill.

iv. be the sole original non-negotiable sea waybill or, if issued in more than one original, be the full set as indicated on the non-negotiable sea waybill.

v. contain terms and conditions of carriage or make reference to another source containing the terms and conditions of carriage (short form or blank back non-negotiable sea waybill). Contents of terms and conditions of carriage will not be examined.

vi. contain no indication that it is subject to a charter party.

b. For the purpose of this article, transhipment means unloading from one vessel and reloading to another vessel during the carriage from the port of loading to the port of discharge stated in the credit.

c. i. A non-negotiable sea waybill may indicate that the goods will or may be transhipped provided that the entire carriage is covered by one and the same non-negotiable sea waybill.

ii. A non-negotiable sea waybill indicating that transhipment will or may take place is acceptable, even if the credit prohibits transhipment, if the goods have been shipped in a container, trailer or LASH barge as evidenced by the non-negotiable sea waybill.

d. Clauses in a non-negotiable sea waybill stating that the carrier reserves the right to tranship will be disregarded.

Changes from UCP 500

- Deletion of "If a Credit calls for", "banks will, unless otherwise stipulated in the Credit, accept a document";
- Deletion of reference to "appears on its face", as this is now referred to solely in sub-article 14 (a) as a general principle covering all stipulated documents;
- Deletion of "or otherwise authenticated", "authentication" and "authenticating" due to the interpretation of signing in article 3;
- Standard wording for the manner in which a transport document is to indicate the name of the carrier and that the transport document must be prepared in a way that it is possible to identify in which capacity the party signing the document does sign – as carrier, master or agent;
- Requirements for shipment on board a named vessel at the port of loading are now combined;
- Requirements in connection with a non-negotiable sea waybill showing a place of receipt or taking in charge different from the port of loading stated in the documentary credit;
- Wording to make it clear that the non-negotiable sea waybill must evidence shipment between the port of loading and the port of discharge stated in the documentary credit;

- Deletion of reference to vessels propelled by sail;
- Deletion of "in all other respects meets the stipulations of the Credit". This provision is not required due to the definition of "Complying presentation" in article 2;
- Transhipment provisions have now been split across three sub-articles to accommodate a general definition for the type of transport covered by the article, the provisions applicable when transhipment is evidenced within the transport document, the effect of transhipment where the documentary credit prohibits such action and the allowance for clauses reserving the right to tranship.

COMMENTARY

This article applies when the documentary credit requires presentation of a non-negotiable sea waybill covering transport by sea from one port to another port.

During the revision process, the Drafting Group compared the content of UCP 500 articles 23 and 24. The comparison highlighted what we all knew, namely that there was no difference in the wording except that whenever the words "bill of lading" appeared in article 23, the words "non-negotiable sea waybill" appeared in article 24. At one point, the Drafting Group combined the two articles into one. However, responses from ICC national committees asserted that it was unwise to combine in one article of the rules a document which is, in most cases, a negotiable document (the bill of lading) and, on the other hand, a document which bears in its title words to the effect that it is non-negotiable (the non-negotiable sea waybill). The decision was then taken to remain with what existed under UCP 500 and to have a separate article for the non-negotiable sea waybill.

Wording to the effect that "If a Credit calls for a non-negotiable sea waybill covering a port-to-port shipment, banks will, unless otherwise stipulated in the Credit, accept a document ..." was considered to be unnecessary. It was decided that the rules should only stipulate the requirements linked to the document rather than referring to what banks will accept, if a credit calls for such a document. Likewise, it was considered unnecessary to repeat "unless otherwise stipulated in the credit", since this, as indicated earlier in the Commentary, is taken care of by the general stipulation "unless expressly modified or excluded by the credit" in article 1.

As is the case for all other transport documents, there is no reference to "on its face" in this article. The decision was made by the Drafting Group that there should be a reference to "on its face" or "on their face" in UCP 600, but that there was only a need for this to appear in one place, sub-article 14 (a).

The deletion of "or otherwise authenticated", "authentication" and "authenticating" in relation to the manner in which non-negotiable sea waybills are signed follows the principle adopted for all of the transport articles. The interpretation of signing in article 3 includes a reference to "... any other mechanical or electronic method of authentication".

Sub-article (a) (i) requires that the name of the carrier be indicated on the non-negotiable sea waybill. This can be by a specific reference within the body of the non-negotiable sea waybill, e.g., "ABC Co. Ltd, the carrier" or by the way the respective document is signed, e.g., "For ABC Co. Ltd as carrier". The manner of signing described here is not exclusive and would include circumstances such as those in which a named agent signs for or on behalf of the [named] carrier.

It should be noted that the manner in which non-negotiable sea waybills indicate the name of the carrier and are to be signed has not changed between UCP 500 and UCP 600. The only exception to the signing requirements occurs when the non-negotiable sea waybill is signed by an agent for or on behalf of the master. In this event the master's name. As explained in the Commentary to article 19, "the transportation industry pointed out it is quite common for agents not to know the name of the master of a vessel at the time the transport document is issued."

As one example of indicating the capacity of the carrier, if a non-negotiable sea waybill is issued by a company called "XYZ SL Ltd" or "XYZ Ltd", it would be difficult to assess whether either company is a carrier. A document checker will only be able to determine that the non-negotiable sea waybill appears to have been issued by the company "XYZ SL Ltd" or "XYZ Ltd", but not the capacity in which the company is acting. Therefore, whatever the name of the company that issued the non-negotiable sea waybill, an indication to the effect that the issuing company or another company is the carrier is required. This requirement will also be fulfilled if the party signing the non-negotiable sea waybill indicates that it is signing "as carrier" or as agent for a named carrier.

To take another example, while it may appear that a non-negotiable sea waybill issued by a company called "ABC Shipping Lines Ltd" is a non-negotiable sea waybill that indicates the name of the carrier, unless the word "carrier" appears on the non-negotiable sea waybill linked to the name of the company, the company name in and of itself will not be sufficient.

Sub-article (a) (i) also goes on to describe what is required by way of signature. The party signing the non-negotiable sea waybill must indicate whether it is signing as carrier, master or agent, and if the party is signing as agent, the name of that agent must be included, as well as the capacity in which it is signing. Therefore, a simple signature on the non-negotiable sea waybill does not suffice. The indication of the capacity of the one signing the non-negotiable sea waybill must also appear in the signature box. However, if the non-negotiable sea waybill shows the name of the issuing company together with the indication "carrier", a simple signature in the signature box with the indication "for and on behalf of [name of the issuing company]" or "for and on behalf of the carrier" or a similar indication would be sufficient.

The rules require that an agent signing the non-negotiable sea waybill must indicate whether it is signing for or on behalf of the carrier or for or on behalf of the master. As mentioned above, the transportation industry pointed out that it is quite common for agents not to know the name of the master of a vessel at the time a non-negotiable sea waybill is issued, and therefore the name of the master should not need to be indicated on the non-negotiable sea waybill. This has been recognized by the rules, which require that the carrier and a named agent be indicated, but has no such requirement for the master's name.

During the revision process, a number of communications were sent between the Drafting Group and representatives of the ICC Transport Commission. As a result it was agreed that the non-negotiable sea waybill is a transport document covering shipment from a port of loading to a port of discharge and that the rules should reflect that position. As a non-negotiable sea waybill covers shipment from a port to a port, the wording that appeared in UCP 500 sub-article 24 (a) (ii) was seen to encourage the presentation of a document that covered pre-carriage of the goods to the port of loading. The wording of this sub-article reads: "If the non-negotiable sea waybill indicates a place of receipt or taking in charge different from the port of loading, the on board notation must also include the port of loading stipulated in the Credit and the name of the vessel on which the goods have been loaded, even if they have been loaded on the vessel named in the non-negotiable sea waybill. This provision also applies whenever loading on board the vessel is indicated by pre-printed wording on the non-negotiable sea waybill."

Where pre-carriage by road, rail or air and shipment by sea is envisaged, the parties should ensure that the credit allows for a transport document to be presented that would be subject to examination under UCP 600 article 19.

The Drafting Group recognized that whilst UCP 600 conveys that the non-negotiable sea waybill is a port-to-port document, there will be occasions when the shipping company or its agent will include reference to a place of receipt or taking in charge that is different from the port of loading. To cover this eventuality, the content of sub-article 21 (a) (ii) reads: "indicate that the goods have been shipped on board a named vessel at the port of loading stated in the credit by:". The emphasis in this condition is that the document checker must be able to determine that the non-negotiable sea waybill appears to indicate that the shipped on board statement (pre-printed wording or by a separate notation) relates to loading on board the named vessel at the port of loading stated in the credit and not to any pre-carriage of the goods between a place of receipt or taking in charge and the port of loading. Unless it is evident from the non-negotiable sea waybill that the shipped on board statement applies to the vessel and the port of loading, the non-negotiable sea waybill will require, as was the case in UCP 500, an on board notation showing the port of loading and the name of the vessel, even if the goods are loaded on the vessel named in the non-negotiable sea waybill. A shipped on board date will be considered to be the date of shipment. When the non-negotiable sea waybill includes an on board notation, the date of the on board notation will be deemed to be the date of shipment whether or not this date is prior to or after the date of issuance of the non-negotiable sea waybill.

When a place of receipt or taking in charge is the same as the port of loading, e.g., place of receipt Hong Kong CY and port of loading Hong Kong, the conclusion given in ICC Opinion R.282 applies, namely, " Using your example where a place of receipt is given as 'Hong Kong CY' and the port of loading is shown as 'Hong Kong', they are to be deemed one and the same place and therefore not subject to the provisions of [UCP 500] sub-Article 23(a)(ii)." This opinion will also apply in respect of sub-article 21 (a) (ii).

The non-negotiable sea waybill must appear to indicate that shipment has been effected from the port of loading to the port of discharge as stated in the documentary credit. Sub-article (a) (iii) refers to this.

Sub-article (a) (iii) states that if a non-negotiable sea waybill does not indicate the port of loading stated in the documentary credit as the port of loading, it must contain an on board notation which indicates the port of loading stated in the documentary credit, the date of shipment and the name of the vessel. The same criteria apply if the non-negotiable sea waybill indicates the qualification "intended" or similar in respect of the port of loading.

An example of where a non-negotiable sea waybill does not indicate the port of loading stated in the documentary credit as the port of loading, would be when the port of loading stated in the documentary credit is shown as the place of receipt, since in the field port of loading it shows the port where transhipment is to occur. The documentary credit requires shipment from Rotterdam to Hong Kong. Sub-article (a) (iii) requires the non-negotiable sea waybill to indicate shipment from the port of loading to the port of discharge stated in the credit.

The non-negotiable sea waybill shows:

Pre-carriage	Moon Lagoon
Place of receipt	Rotterdam
Ocean Vessel	Sun Lagoon
Port of Loading	Dubai
Port of Discharge	Hong Kong

The non-negotiable sea waybill will require, according to sub-article (a) (iii), an on board notation showing the vessel Moon Lagoon, the port of loading Rotterdam and the on board date.

The above example is a common structure of a non-negotiable sea waybill today. The shipping company or its agent seeks to describe the entire journey of the goods and, as a result, the data does not appear in corresponding boxes on the non-negotiable sea waybill. The example is showing shipment from Rotterdam to Hong Kong with transhipment in Dubai.

A non-negotiable sea waybill evidencing a place of final destination different from the port of discharge as stated in the documentary credit would be acceptable.

Sub-article (a) (iv) continues to stress the UCP 500 position that the non-negotiable sea waybill must appear to be the sole original non-negotiable sea waybill that has been issued or, if it indicates that it has been issued in more than one original, all of the stated originals must be presented unless the documentary credit indicates the disposal instruction for one or more of the original non-negotiable sea waybills.

The non-negotiable sea waybill usually contains the terms and conditions of carriage. However, as this is not always the case, sub-article (a) (v) allows for a non-negotiable sea waybill to make reference to a source other than the document itself to determine these terms and conditions. In this respect, a non-negotiable sea waybill that contains a reference to a source other than itself has generally been described as a "short form" or "blank back" non-negotiable sea waybill. Banks are not to examine the contents of the terms and conditions of carriage.

Sub-article (a) (vi) stipulates that the non-negotiable sea waybill must not contain an indication that it is subject to a charter party. The term "no indication" means that a non-negotiable sea waybill that bears any indication that it is subject to a charter party would not be acceptable under this article. As examples of "no indication", the non-negotiable sea waybill may state "to be used with charter parties" or it could contain the following data: "freight payable as per charter party" or "charter party contract number ABC123".

Since sail boats are rarely, if ever, used for transportation of goods in international trade, it was decided that a clause prohibiting presentation of a non-negotiable sea waybill indicating that the carrying vessel is propelled by sail only was no longer necessary.

Sub-article (b) provides a definition of transhipment when a non-negotiable sea waybill is required.

Sub-article (c) (i) explains that transhipment must be evidenced within one and the same non-negotiable sea waybill. Separate documents covering each leg of a journey would not be acceptable.

Sub-article (c) (ii) recognizes the shipping industry practice that transhipment often occurs when goods are shipped in containers, trailers or LASH barges by stating that this is allowed even if prohibited by the documentary credit. The only way that an applicant can completely prohibit transhipment would be to state that transhipment is prohibited *and* that sub-article 21 (c) (ii) is not applicable or is excluded.

Sub-article (d) recognizes that a statement on a non-negotiable sea waybill indicating that the carrier reserves the right to do something, in this case, tranship, does not imply that it has or will do so and is an acceptable condition.

Cross-references within UCP 600

- Article 2 – definition of "Credit";
- Article 3 concerning interpretation of signatures;
- Article 3 concerning interpretation for determining periods of shipment;
- Sub-article 14 (c) – Standard for Examination of Documents – on the presentation period;
- Sub-article 14 (d) – Standard for Examination of Documents – on data not being in conflict;
- Sub-article 14 (e) – Standard for Examination of Documents – on goods description on documents other than the commercial invoice;
- Sub-article 14 (j) – Standard for Examination of Documents – on addresses of the applicant as consignee or notify party;
- Sub-article 14 (k) – Standard for Examination of Documents – on the shipper or consignor indicated on a document;
- Sub-article 14 (l) – Standard for Examination of Documents – on issuance of transport documents other than by the carrier, master, owner or charterer;
- Article 17 – Original Documents and Copies;
- Article 26 – "On Deck", "Shipper's Load and Count", "Said by Shipper to Contain" and Charges Additional to Freight;
- Article 27 – Clean Transport Document;
- Article 29 – Extension of Expiry Date or Last Day for Presentation – on non-extension of latest shipment date;
- Article 31 – Partial Drawings or Shipments;
- Article 32 – Instalment Drawings or Shipments;
- Article 34 – Disclaimer on Effectiveness of Documents.

Article 22

Charter Party Bill of Lading

a. A bill of lading, however named, containing an indication that it is subject to a charter party (charter party bill of lading), must appear to:

i. be signed by:

- the master or a named agent for or on behalf of the master, or
- the owner or a named agent for or on behalf of the owner, or
- the charterer or a named agent for or on behalf of the charterer.

Any signature by the master, owner, charterer or agent must be identified as that of the master, owner, charterer or agent.

Any signature by an agent must indicate whether the agent has signed for or on behalf of the master, owner or charterer.

An agent signing for or on behalf of the owner or charterer must indicate the name of the owner or charterer.

ii. indicate that the goods have been shipped on board a named vessel at the port of loading stated in the credit by:

- pre-printed wording, or
- an on board notation indicating the date on which the goods have been shipped on board.

The date of issuance of the charter party bill of lading will be deemed to be the date of shipment unless the charter party bill of lading contains an on board notation indicating the date of shipment, in which case the date stated in the on board notation will be deemed to be the date of shipment.

iii. indicate shipment from the port of loading to the port of discharge stated in the credit. The port of discharge may also be shown as a range of ports or a geographical area, as stated in the credit.

iv. be the sole original charter party bill of lading or, if issued in more than one original, be the full set as indicated on the charter party bill of lading.

b. A bank will not examine charter party contracts, even if they are required to be presented by the terms of the credit.

Changes from UCP 500

- Deletion of "If a Credit calls for", "banks will, unless otherwise stipulated in the Credit, accept a document";
- Deletion of reference to "appears on its face", as this is now referred to solely in sub-article 14 (a) as a general principle covering all stipulated documents;
- Deletion of "or otherwise authenticated", "authentication" and "authenticating" due to the interpretation of signing in article 3;
- Addition of a charterer and an agent of the charterer to the list of persons who may sign a charter party bill of lading;
- Deletion of the requirement for the name of the master to be stated in cases where an agent of the master signs;
- Deletion of the clause which states that charter party bills of lading must not indicate that the carrying vessel is propelled by sail only;
- A charter party bill of lading may now show as port of discharge a range of ports or a geographical area if that range or geographical area has been stated as the port of discharge in the documentary credit. This rule was previously covered by paragraph 106 in the ISBP, ICC Publication No. 645;
- Deletion of "does or does not indicate the name of the carrier". This provision was not replicated in UCP 600 because its wording does not provide a definitive rule. In any event, whether or not the charter party bill of lading includes the name of the carrier has no effect in determining compliance of the document with the documentary credit or UCP 600;
- Deletion of "in all other respects meets the stipulations of the Credit". This provision is not required due to the definition of "Complying presentation" in article 2.

Commentary

This article applies when the documentary credit requires or permits presentation of a charter party bill of lading and a charter party bill of lading is presented. A charter party bill of lading is a bill of lading containing an indication that it is subject to a charter party.

Wording to the effect that "If a Credit calls for or permits a charter party bill of lading, banks will, unless otherwise stipulated in the Credit, accept a document ..." was considered to be unnecessary. It was decided that the rules should only stipulate the requirements linked to the document rather than referring to what banks will accept, if a credit calls for such a document. Likewise, it was considered unnecessary to repeat "unless otherwise stipulated in the credit", since this, as indicated earlier in the Commentary, is taken care of by the general stipulation "unless expressly modified or excluded by the credit" in article 1.

As is the case for all other transport documents, there is no reference to "on its face" in this article. The decision was made by the Drafting Group that there should be a reference to "on its face" or "on their face" in UCP 600, but that there was only a need for this to appear in one place, sub-article 14 (a).

The deletion of "or otherwise authenticated", "authentication" and "authenticating" in relation to the manner in which charter party bills of lading are signed follows the principle adopted for all of the transport articles. The interpretation of signing in article 3 includes a reference to "... any other mechanical or electronic method of authentication".

Sub-article (a) (i) outlines the signing requirements for a charter party bill of lading, indicating that it may be signed by the master, the owner or the charterer, or an agent of the master, the owner or the charterer. If the charter party bill of lading is signed by the master, owner or charterer, the signature must be identifiable as that of one of these parties. If signed by an agent, that agent's name must be stated, and the agent must state for whom he has signed and, if he has signed for or on behalf of the owner or the charterer, the name of the owner or charterer must be stated.

However, if the charter party bill of lading is signed by an agent for or on behalf of the master, the master's name need not be stated. As explained in the Commentary to article 19, "the transportation industry pointed out it is quite common for agents not to know the name of the master of a vessel at the time the transport document is issued." This has been recognized by the rules, which require an agent to state his own name and, only if signing for or on behalf of the owner or charterer, to indicate the name of the owner or charterer.

The provision in UCP 500 sub-article 25 (a) (iii) that the charter party bill of lading does or does not indicate the name of the carrier was not replicated in UCP 600 because its wording does not provide a definitive rule. In any event, whether or not the charter party bill of lading includes the name of the carrier has no effect in determining compliance of the document with the documentary credit or UCP 600.

The term "charterer" was included at the request of the ICC Transport Commission, whose members noted that it is a growing practice for charterers to either sign or become involved in the creation of charter party bills of lading.

Similar to other transport articles involving transportation by sea, sub-article (a) (ii) requires that the charter party bill of lading indicate that the goods have been shipped on board a named vessel at the port of loading stated in the documentary credit. The shipped on board date will be deemed to be the date of shipment. The words "at the port of loading stated in the credit" have been specifically included to emphasize that banks must be able to determine from the charter party bill of lading, not only that the goods were shipped within the latest shipment date stated in the documentary credit, but also that there is evidence that the date of shipment relates to shipment from the port of loading stated in the documentary credit and not from any other place of receipt or taking in charge evidenced within the charter party bill of lading.

Sub-article (a) (ii) also describes the manner in which banks will determine that the goods have been shipped on board, i.e., by pre-printed wording or by an on board notation. When the charter party bill of lading includes an on board notation, the date of the on board notation will be deemed to be the date of shipment whether or not this date is prior to or after the date of issuance of the charter party bill of lading.

The charter party bill of lading must appear to indicate that shipment has been effected from the port of loading to the port of discharge as stated in the documentary credit. Sub-article (a) (iii) refers to this.

Recognizing there is a difference between transportation under charter party contracts and by liner vessels, it was decided that whilst the charter party bill of lading must show a named port or ports of loading and port or ports of discharge, it is acceptable if it shows the port or ports of discharge exactly as stated in the documentary credit, even if the documentary credit shows a range of ports or geographical area as the required port of discharge, e.g., "any Chinese port".

Sub-article (a) (iv) continues to stress the UCP 500 position that the charter party bill of lading must appear to be the sole original charter party bill of lading that has been issued or, if it indicates that it has been issued in more than one original, all of the stated originals must be presented unless the documentary credit indicates the disposal instruction for one or more of the original charter party bills of lading.

Since sail boats are rarely, if ever, used for transportation of goods in international trade, it was decided that a clause prohibiting presentation of a charter party bill of lading indicating that the carrying vessel is propelled by sail only was no longer necessary.

Sub-article (b) states that banks should continue to discourage any requirement for presentation of a charter party contract under a documentary credit.

Cross-references in UCP 600

- Article 2 – definition of "Credit";
- Article 3 concerning interpretation of signatures;
- Article 3 concerning interpretation for determining periods of shipment;
- Sub-article 14 (c) – Standard for Examination of Documents – on the presentation period;
- Sub-article 14 (d) – Standard for Examination of Documents – on data not being in conflict;
- Sub-article 14 (e) – Standard for Examination of Documents – on goods description on documents other than the commercial invoice;
- Sub-article 14 (j) – Standard for Examination of Documents – on addresses of the applicant as consignee or notify party;
- Sub-article 14 (k) – Standard for Examination of Documents – on shipper or consignor indicated on a document;
- Sub-article 14 (l) – Standard for Examination of Documents – on issuance of transport documents other than by the carrier, master, owner or charterer;
- Article 17 – Original Documents and Copies;
- Article 26 – "On Deck", "Shipper's Load and Count", "Said by Shipper to Contain" and Charges Additional to Freight;
- Article 27 – Clean Transport Document;
- Article 29 – Extension of Expiry Date or Last Day for Presentation – on non-extension of latest shipment date;
- Article 31 – Partial Drawings or Shipments;
- Article 32 – Instalment Drawings or Shipments;
- Article 34 – Disclaimer on Effectiveness of Documents.

Article 23

Air Transport Document

a. An air transport document, however named, must appear to:

i. indicate the name of the carrier and be signed by:

- the carrier, or
- a named agent for or on behalf of the carrier.

Any signature by the carrier or agent must be identified as that of the carrier or agent.

Any signature by an agent must indicate that the agent has signed for or on behalf of the carrier.

ii. indicate that the goods have been accepted for carriage.

iii. indicate the date of issuance. This date will be deemed to be the date of shipment unless the air transport document contains a specific notation of the actual date of shipment, in which case the date stated in the notation will be deemed to be the date of shipment.

Any other information appearing on the air transport document relative to the flight number and date will not be considered in determining the date of shipment.

iv. indicate the airport of departure and the airport of destination stated in the credit.

v. be the original for consignor or shipper, even if the credit stipulates a full set of originals.

vi. contain terms and conditions of carriage or make reference to another source containing the terms and conditions of carriage. Contents of terms and conditions of carriage will not be examined.

b. For the purpose of this article, transhipment means unloading from one aircraft and reloading to another aircraft during the carriage from the airport of departure to the airport of destination stated in the credit.

c. i. An air transport document may indicate that the goods will or may be transhipped, provided that the entire carriage is covered by one and the same air transport document.

ii. An air transport document indicating that transhipment will or may take place is acceptable, even if the credit prohibits transhipment.

Changes from UCP 500

- Deletion of "If a Credit calls for", "banks will, unless otherwise stipulated in the Credit, accept a document";
- Deletion of reference to "appears on its face", as this is now referred to solely in sub-article 14 (a) as a general principle covering all stipulated documents;
- Deletion of "or otherwise authenticated", "authentication" and "authenticating" due to the interpretation of signing in article 3;
- Specific notation that the actual date of shipment on the air transport document will be considered to be the date of shipment, whether or not there is a requirement in the documentary credit for such a notation;
- Deletion of "in all other respects meets the stipulations of the Credit". This provision is not required due to the definition of "Complying presentation" in article 2;
- Transhipment provisions have now been split between two sub-articles to accommodate a general definition for the type of transport covered by the article, the provisions applicable when transhipment is evidenced within the transport document and the effect of transhipment when the documentary credit prohibits such action.

Commentary

This article applies when the documentary credit requires the presentation of an air transport document, e.g., an air consignment note or air waybill.

Wording to the effect that "If a Credit calls for an air transport document, banks will, unless otherwise stipulated in the Credit, accept a document ..." was considered to be unnecessary. It was decided that the rules should only stipulate the requirements linked to the document rather than referring to what banks will accept, if a credit calls for such a document. Likewise, it was considered unnecessary to repeat "unless otherwise stipulated in the credit", since this, as indicated earlier in the Commentary, is taken care of by the general stipulation "unless expressly modified or excluded by the credit" in article 1.

As is the case for all other transport documents, there is no reference to "on its face" in this article. The decision was made by the Drafting Group that there should be a reference to "on its face" or "on their face" in UCP 600, but that there was only a need for this to appear in one place, sub-article 14 (a).

The deletion of "or otherwise authenticated", "authentication" and "authenticating" in relation to the manner in which air transport documents are signed follows the principle adopted for all of the transport articles. The interpretation of signing in article 3 includes a reference to "... any other mechanical or electronic method of authentication".

Sub-article (a) (i) requires that the name of the carrier be indicated on the air transport document. This can be by a specific reference to this capacity within the body of the air transport document, e.g., "ABC Co. Ltd, the carrier" or by the way the respective document is signed, e.g., "For ABC Co. Ltd as carrier". The manner of signing described here is not exclusive and would include circumstances such as those in which a named agent signs for or on behalf of the [named] carrier.

It should be noted that the manner in which air transport documents indicate the name of the carrier and are to be signed has not changed between UCP 500 and UCP 600.

Sub-article (a) (ii) repeats the UCP 500 position that the air transport document must indicate that the goods have been accepted for carriage.

The Drafting Group could not think of any reason why a separate notation of a date of dispatch should only override the issuance date when a separate notation is called for by the documentary credit, as was the case under UCP 500.

Therefore, as stated in sub-article (a) (iii), a notation of the actual date of dispatch will be taken to be the date of shipment whether or not such notation is called for in the documentary credit. In the absence of a notation and where the documentary credit does not request a notation of the actual date of dispatch, the date of issuance of the air transport document will be taken to be the date of shipment. A notation could be a stamp or a specifically designated area within the document. The completion of any other pre-printed box or field on an air transport document with a flight number and date does not constitute a notation for the purpose of determining the date of shipment.

UCP 500 sub-article 27 (a) (iii) stated that information contained in the box designated "For Carrier Use Only" should be disregarded in determining the date of shipment. Under sub-article (a) (iii), it should be noted that any information concerning the flight date, including a notation as described above, will be disregarded for the purpose of determining the date of shipment.

The air transport document must appear to indicate that dispatch has been effected from the airport of departure to the airport of destination as stated in the documentary credit. Sub-article (a) (iv) refers to this.

Sub-article (a) (v) states that a presentation must include an original air transport document that appears to be the one for the consignor or shipper. A documentary credit should not call for a full set of original air transport documents, as this kind of document is not issued in this manner. A request for a full set will be fulfilled by the presentation of an "original for consignor or shipper".

The air transport document usually contains the terms and conditions of carriage. However, as this is not always the case, sub-article (a) (v) allows for an air transport document to make reference to a source other than the document itself to determine these terms and conditions. Banks are not to examine the contents of the terms and conditions of carriage.

Sub-article (b) provides a definition of transhipment when an air transport document is required.

Sub-article (c) (i) explains that transhipment must be evidenced within one and the same air transport document. Separate documents covering each leg of a journey would not be acceptable.

Sub-article (c) (ii) recognizes the air transport industry practice that transhipment often occurs in air transport by stating that this is allowed even if prohibited by the documentary credit. The only way that an applicant can completely prohibit transhipment would be to state that transhipment is prohibited *and* that sub-article 23 (c) (ii) is not applicable or is excluded.

Cross-references in UCP 600

- Article 2 – definition of "Credit";
- Article 3 concerning interpretation of signatures;
- Article 3 concerning interpretation for determining periods of shipment;
- Sub-article 14 (c) – Standard for Examination of Documents – on the presentation period;
- Sub-article 14 (d) – Standard for Examination of Documents – on data not being in conflict;
- Sub-article 14 (e) – Standard for Examination of Documents – on goods description on documents other than the commercial invoice;
- Sub-article 14 (j) – Standard for Examination of Documents – on addresses of the applicant as consignee or notify party;
- Sub-article 14 (k) – Standard for Examination of Documents – on shipper or consignor indicated on a document;
- Sub-article 14 (l) – Standard for Examination of Documents – on issuance of transport documents other than by the carrier, master, owner or charterer;
- Article 17 – Original Documents and Copies;

- Article 26 – "On Deck", "Shipper's Load and Count", "Said by Shipper to Contain" and Charges Additional to Freight – on charges additional to freight;
- Article 29 – Extension of Expiry Date or Last Day for Presentation – on non-extension of latest shipment date;
- Article 31 – Partial Drawings or Shipments;
- Article 32 – Instalment Drawings or Shipments;
- Article 34 – Disclaimer on Effectiveness of Documents.

ARTICLE 24

Road, Rail or Inland Waterway Transport Documents

a. A road, rail or inland waterway transport document, however named, must appear to:

   i. indicate the name of the carrier and:

   - be signed by the carrier or a named agent for or on behalf of the carrier, or
   - indicate receipt of the goods by signature, stamp or notation by the carrier or a named agent for or on behalf of the carrier.

   Any signature, stamp or notation of receipt of the goods by the carrier or agent must be identified as that of the carrier or agent.

   Any signature, stamp or notation of receipt of the goods by the agent must indicate that the agent has signed or acted for or on behalf of the carrier.

   If a rail transport document does not identify the carrier, any signature or stamp of the railway company will be accepted as evidence of the document being signed by the carrier.

   ii. indicate the date of shipment or the date the goods have been received for shipment, dispatch or carriage at the place stated in the credit. Unless the transport document contains a dated reception stamp, an indication of the date of receipt or a date of shipment, the date of issuance of the transport document will be deemed to be the date of shipment.

   iii. indicate the place of shipment and the place of destination stated in the credit.

b. i. A road transport document must appear to be the original for consignor or shipper or bear no marking indicating for whom the document has been prepared.

   ii. A rail transport document marked "duplicate" will be accepted as an original.

   iii. A rail or inland waterway transport document will be accepted as an original whether marked as an original or not.

c. In the absence of an indication on the transport document as to the number of originals issued, the number presented will be deemed to constitute a full set.

d. For the purpose of this article, transhipment means unloading from one means of conveyance and reloading to another means of conveyance, within the same mode of transport, during the carriage from the place of shipment, dispatch or carriage to the place of destination stated in the credit.

e. i. A road, rail or inland waterway transport document may indicate that the goods will or may be transhipped provided that the entire carriage is covered by one and the same transport document.

ii. A road, rail or inland waterway transport document indicating that transhipment will or may take place is acceptable, even if the credit prohibits transhipment.

Changes from UCP 500

- Deletion of "If a Credit calls for", "banks will, unless otherwise stipulated in the Credit, accept a document";
- Deletion of reference to "appears on its face", as this is now referred to solely in sub-article 14 (a) as a general principle covering all stipulated documents;
- Deletion of "or otherwise authenticated", "authentication" and "authenticating" due to the interpretation of signing in article 3;
- Addition of a separate paragraph to cover the identification of carriers on railway bills;
- Addition of specific rules covering the acceptability of road, rail or inland waterway transport documents as originals;
- Deletion of phrase "reception stamp or other indication of receipt" and restructuring of the wording in sub-article (a) (ii) to incorporate a reference, not only to a reception stamp (as mentioned in sub-article 28 (a) (ii) of UCP 500), but also an indication of the date of receipt or date of shipment;
- Deletion of "in all other respects meets the stipulations of the Credit". This provision is not required due to the definition of "Complying presentation" in article 2;
- Change in the definition of "transhipment" from being unloading and reloading in different modes of transport to unloading and reloading within the same mode of transport.

COMMENTARY

This article applies when the documentary credit requires the presentation of road, rail or inland waterway transport documents.

The transport documents covered by this article are not exclusively subject to international legislation, construction or content. For example, whilst in Europe a CMR transport document will usually be issued covering road transport, in other parts of the world such a road transport document can be issued solely on the letterhead of a freight forwarder or trucking company.

Wording to the effect that "If a Credit calls for a road, rail or inland waterway transport document, banks will, unless otherwise stipulated in the Credit, accept a document ..." was considered to be unnecessary. It was decided that the rules should only stipulate the requirements linked to the document rather than referring to what banks will accept, if a credit calls for such a document. Likewise, it was considered unnecessary to repeat "unless otherwise stipulated in the credit", since this, as indicated earlier in the Commentary, is taken care of by the general stipulation "unless expressly modified or excluded by the credit" in article 1.

As is the case for all other transport documents, there is no reference to "on its face" in this article. The decision was made by the Drafting Group that there should be a reference to "on its face" or "on their face" in UCP 600, but that there was only a need for this to appear in one place, sub-article 14 (a).

The deletion of "or otherwise authenticated", "authentication" and "authenticating" in relation to the manner in which these documents are signed follows the principle adopted for all of the transport articles. The interpretation of signing in article 3 includes a reference to "... any other mechanical or electronic method of authentication".

Sub-article (a) (i) requires that the name of the carrier be indicated on the transport document. This can be by a specific reference to this capacity within the body of the transport document, e.g., "ABC Co. Ltd, the carrier" or by the way the respective document is signed, e.g., "For ABC Co. Ltd as carrier". The manner of signing described here is not exclusive and would include circumstances such as those in which a named agent signs for or on behalf of the [named] carrier.

It should be noted that the manner in which these transport documents indicate the name of the carrier and are to be signed has not changed between UCP 500 and UCP 600.

In recognition of transport industry practice for the issuance of rail waybills, an exception has been made for a rail waybill to be accepted bearing any signature or stamp which appears to be that of a railway company as evidence of one being signed by the carrier. Otherwise, the transport document must either be signed by the carrier or a named agent of the carrier, or evidence the receipt of the goods by the carrier or agent by a stamp or a notation, always indicating the capacity of the carrier or the agent, as the case may be.

The change in wording appearing in sub-article (a) (ii) reflects the manner, other than a date of issuance of the transport document, in which shipment may be evidenced across the three modes of transport covered by this article.

The same sub-article reflects a similar position for road, rail or inland waterway documents as the one that appears in sub-article 23 (a) (iii) covering air transport documents, i.e., that the date of issuance will be deemed to be the date of shipment unless, in the case of this article, there is a dated reception stamp, date of receipt or date of shipment appearing on the transport document.

The transport document must appear to indicate that shipment, dispatch or carriage has been effected from the place of shipment to the place of destination as stated in the documentary credit. Sub-article (a) (iii) refers to this.

One of the criticisms of UCP 500 article 28 – and why a number of ICC national committees requested that this article be split into three separate articles – was that the rules were applicable to all three types of transport and there were no variations according to the mode of transport used. This has been rectified in this article. Sub-article (b) contains provisions applicable to one or more modes of transport. The provisions reflect transport industry practice with regard to road, rail or inland waterway and, in some cases, shows the different treatment that each receives as a result of these practices.

For example, even if there is no indication that the document presented is actually the consignor or shipper's receipt for the goods, a road transport document that appears to be an original is acceptable as long as it does not appear to have been prepared for someone other than the consignor or shipper.

International rail waybills in some parts of the world are marked "Duplicate" and are acceptable as original railway bills.

Documents in general need not be marked "Original" to serve as originals as long as they appear to be original. Rail and inland waterway transport documents do not normally carry an indication of "original". The basis on which they will be considered to be original is if they comply with sub-articles 17 (b) and (c) or with the provisions of sub-article (b) (ii) for rail or (iii) for rail or inland waterway.

As it is not normal for the transport documents covered by this article to indicate the number of originals that have been issued, a bank will consider the number of transport documents presented as being the number of originals issued.

Obviously, when the document does indicate that a certain number of originals have been issued, then the full set as indicated on the transport document must be presented. In this respect, refer to sub-article (c).

The definition of transhipment in UCP 500 sub-article 28 (c) was actually a definition of transhipment in circumstances in which more than one mode of transport was utilized. This article in UCP 600 covers transportation by road or rail or inland waterway and not by a mixture of these modes of transport. Therefore, transhipment can only be defined in sub-article (d) as unloading and reloading within the same mode of transport.

Sub-article (d) provides a definition of transhipment when a road, rail or inland waterway transport document is required.

Sub-article (e) (i) explains that transhipment must be evidenced within one and the same transport document. Separate documents covering each leg of a journey would not be acceptable.

Sub-article (e) (ii) recognizes that there are many possibilities in the way that goods are transported inland. Consequently, it was decided to retain the UCP 500 position that transhipment is allowed even if prohibited by the documentary credit. The only way that an applicant can completely prohibit transhipment would be to state that transhipment is prohibited *and* that sub-article 24 (e) (ii) is not applicable or is excluded.

Cross-references in UCP 600

- Article 2 – Definition of "Credit"
- Article 3 concerning interpretation of signatures;
- Article 3 concerning interpretation for determining periods of shipment;
- Sub-article 14 (c) – Standard for Examination of Documents – on the presentation period;
- Sub-article 14 (d) – Standard for Examination of Documents – on data not being in conflict;
- Sub-article 14 (e) – Standard for Examination of Documents – on goods description on documents other than the commercial invoice;
- Sub-article 14 (j) – Standard for Examination of Documents – on addresses of the applicant as consignee or notify party;
- Sub-article 14 (k) – Standard for Examination of Documents – on shipper or consignor indicated on a document;

- Sub-article 14 (l) – Standard for Examination of Documents – on issuance of transport documents other than by the carrier, master, owner or charterer;
- Article 17 – Original Documents and Copies;
- Article 26 – "On Deck", "Shipper's Load and Count", "Said by Shipper to Contain" and Charges Additional to Freight – (as applicable to the type of transport);
- Article 29 – Extension of Expiry Date or Last Day for Presentation – on non-extension of latest shipment date;
- Article 31 – Partial Drawings or Shipments;
- Article 32 – Instalment Drawings or Shipments;
- Article 34 – Disclaimer on Effectiveness of Documents.

ARTICLE 25

Courier Receipt, Post Receipt or Certificate of Posting

a. A courier receipt, however named, evidencing receipt of goods for transport, must appear to:

   i. indicate the name of the courier service and be stamped or signed by the named courier service at the place from which the credit states the goods are to be shipped; and

   ii. indicate a date of pickup or of receipt or wording to this effect. This date will be deemed to be the date of shipment.

b. A requirement that courier charges are to be paid or prepaid may be satisfied by a transport document issued by a courier service evidencing that courier charges are for the account of a party other than the consignee.

c. A post receipt or certificate of posting, however named, evidencing receipt of goods for transport, must appear to be stamped or signed and dated at the place from which the credit states the goods are to be shipped. This date will be deemed to be the date of shipment.

CHANGES FROM UCP 500

- Deletion of "If a Credit calls for", "banks will, unless otherwise stipulated in the Credit, accept a document";
- Deletion of reference to "appears on its face", as this is now referred to solely in sub-article 14 (a) as a general principle covering all stipulated documents;
- Deletion of "or otherwise authenticated" due to the interpretation of signing in article 3;
- Change of the phrase "stamped, signed or otherwise authenticated" to read "stamped or signed";
- Deletion of reference to "(unless the Credit specifically calls for a document issued by a named Courier/Service, banks will accept a document issued by any Courier/Service)";
- Deletion of reference to "expedited delivery service";
- Deletion of "in all other respects meets the stipulations of the Credit". This provision is not required due to the definition of "Complying presentation" in article 2.

Commentary

This article applies when the documentary credit requires the presentation of a courier receipt, post receipt or certificate of posting evidencing receipt of goods for transport.

Wording to the effect that "If a Credit calls for a post receipt or certificate of posting [or a document issued by a courier or expedited delivery service], banks will, unless otherwise stipulated in the Credit, accept a document ..." was considered to be unnecessary. It was decided that the rules should only stipulate the requirements linked to the document rather than referring to what banks will accept, if a credit calls for such a document. Likewise, it was considered unnecessary to repeat "unless otherwise stipulated in the credit", since this, as indicated earlier in the Commentary, is taken care of by the general stipulation "unless expressly modified or excluded by the credit" in article 1.

As is the case for all other transport documents, there is no reference to "on its face" in this article. The decision was made by the Drafting Group that there should be a reference to "on its face" or "on their face" in UCP 600, but there was only a need for this to appear in one place, sub-article 14 (a).

The deletion of "or otherwise authenticated" in relation to the manner in which these documents are signed follows the principle that has been adopted for all of the transport articles. The interpretation of signing in article 3 includes a reference to "... any other mechanical or electronic method of authentication".

The order of this article has been changed to reflect that courier is a more likely form of transport of goods than post. UCP 500 sub-article 29 (b) referred, not only to the use of a courier, but also to an expedited delivery service. However, in international trade, expedited delivery service is not a term used by companies transporting goods. Sub-article (a), therefore, refers to courier only.

The Drafting Group did not deem it necessary that this sub-article contain part of the wording that appeared in UCP 500 sub-article 29 (b) (i). This wording, "(unless the Credit specifically calls for a document issued by a named Courier/Service, banks will accept a document issued by any Courier/Service)", was seen to be covered by the principle that any issuer is acceptable unless a specific courier service was named in the documentary credit.

Sub-article (b) reflects part of the content of UCP 500 sub-article 33 (b) that was applicable to dispatch by courier. It takes account of the fact that courier charges may not be paid at the time of receipt of the goods by the courier, but rather through an account the sender may hold with the courier company. This is no different from how freight charges are paid by shippers under any other mode of transport. This account may allow a number of divisions of a company to bill the courier cost centrally, or may allow another (unrelated) sender to bill the fee to that account. Accounts are normally settled with the courier company on a monthly or quarterly basis.

Similar to the wording in sub-article (a), sub-article (c) also makes reference to "evidencing receipt of goods for transport".

Cross-references in UCP 600

- Article 2 – Definition of "Credit";
- Article 3 concerning interpretation of signatures;
- Article 3 concerning interpretation for determining periods of shipment;
- Sub-article 14 (c) – Standard for Examination of Documents – on the presentation period;
- Sub-article 14 (d) – Standard for Examination of Documents – on data not being in conflict;
- Sub-article 14 (e) – Standard for Examination of Documents – on goods description on documents other than the commercial invoice;
- Sub-article 14 (j) – Standard for Examination of Documents – on addresses of the applicant as consignee or notify party;
- Sub-article 14 (k) – Standard for Examination of Documents – on shipper or consignor indicated on a document;
- Article 17 – Original Documents and Copies;
- Article 29 – Extension of Expiry Date or Last Day for Presentation – on non-extension of latest shipment date;
- Article 31 – Partial Drawings or Shipments;
- Article 32 – Instalment Drawings or Shipments;
- Article 34 – Disclaimer on Effectiveness of Documents.

Article 26

"On Deck", "Shipper's Load and Count", "Said by Shipper to Contain" and Charges Additional to Freight

a. A transport document must not indicate that the goods are or will be loaded on deck. A clause on a transport document stating that the goods may be loaded on deck is acceptable.

b. A transport document bearing a clause such as "shipper's load and count" and "said by shipper to contain" is acceptable.

c. A transport document may bear a reference, by stamp or otherwise, to charges additional to the freight.

Changes from UCP 500

- Deletion of "Unless otherwise stipulated in the Credit, banks will accept a transport document which";
- Deletion of reference to "in the case of carriage by sea";
- Deletion of "on the face thereof";
- Deletion of "or words of similar effect";
- Removal of UCP 500 sub-article 31 (iii) in respect of the consignor of the goods to appear on a transport document;
- Insertion of UCP 500 sub-article 33 (d).

Commentary

As is the case for other articles, the words "Unless otherwise stipulated in the Credit" have been deleted. Article 1 allows for a rule to be modified or excluded by the terms and conditions of the documentary credit. Likewise, the words "in the case of carriage by sea" were deleted, as the Drafting Group considered the term "on deck" to refer solely to carriage by sea and believed that it did not, therefore, need amplification as to the intent of the rule.

Sub-article (a) reconfirms the UCP 500 position that a transport document may contain a provision to the effect that the goods may be loaded on deck, but that the document would be unacceptable if it were to state that the goods have been or will be loaded on deck. When it is known that the type of goods to be shipped may give rise to goods being loaded on deck, the terms and conditions of the documentary credit should cater for this.

In line with the comments made under sub-article 14 (a) – Standard for Examination of Documents – the wording "on the face thereof" has been removed. The wording in sub-article (b) has been further simplified, as the Drafting Group felt that it was not necessary to leave in the wording "or words of similar effect", since the term "a clause such as" is sufficient to emphasize that other examples would also fall under this rule.

UCP 500 sub-article 33 (d) has been moved to this article, which refers to clauses or notations appearing on a transport document. Most of UCP 500 article 33 has been removed. It was not considered necessary, since experience showed that there had not been instances in which banks queried terms related to freight payments that have been or are to be made. Banks' only concern was linked to costs additional to the regular freight charges.

UCP 500 sub-article 31 (iii) ("indicates as the consignor of the goods a party other than the Beneficiary of the Credit") was moved to sub-article 14 (k) and widened in scope, as it was thought best to have this as an item falling under Standard for Examination of Documents.

Cross-references within UCP 600

- Articles 19–25 – covering the transport documents of the UCP;
- Sub-article 14 (k) Standard for Examination of Documents.

ARTICLE 27

Clean Transport Document

A bank will only accept a clean transport document. A clean transport document is one bearing no clause or notation expressly declaring a defective condition of the goods or their packaging. The word "clean" need not appear on a transport document, even if a credit has a requirement for that transport document to be "clean on board".

CHANGES FROM UCP 500

- Deletion of sub-article 32 (b);
- Deletion of sub-article 32 (c);
- Inclusion of a rule that the word "clean" need not appear on a transport document.

COMMENTARY

The main reason for redrafting this article related to the need to create a definitive rule for a clean transport document, i.e., "A bank will only accept a clean transport document."

This article also seeks to remove any ambiguity that existed in documentary credits subject to UCP 500, which led many document examiners to believe that the word "clean" needed to appear on a transport document when the credit called, for example, for a "clean" on board bill of lading or one marked "clean on board". This article makes it quite clear that this is not the case.

ISBP, ICC Publication No. 645, sought to reach this position through the wording that appeared in paragraphs 91, 112, 135 and 161. Paragraph 91, which is representative of the wording, stated, "The word 'clean' need not appear on a bill of lading even though the credit may require a 'clean on board bill of lading' or one marked 'clean on board.'" This has now been removed from the updated version of ISBP (ICC Publication No. 681) for the more definitive and all-encompassing statement "The word 'clean' need not appear on a transport document, even if a credit has a requirement for that transport document to be 'clean on board.'"

Each transport document is considered to be clean, unless it bears an express clause or notation indicating that either the condition of the goods or their packaging is defective. When it is known that the type of goods to be shipped or their packaging may give rise to a clause or notation, the terms and conditions of the documentary credit should cater for this.

Cross-references in UCP 600

- Article 2 – definition of "Credit";
- Articles 19–25 – covering the transport documents of the UCP.

Article 28

Insurance Document and Coverage

a. An insurance document, such as an insurance policy, an insurance certificate or a declaration under an open cover, must appear to be issued and signed by an insurance company, an underwriter or their agents or their proxies.

   Any signature by an agent or proxy must indicate whether the agent or proxy has signed for or on behalf of the insurance company or underwriter.

b. When the insurance document indicates that it has been issued in more than one original, all originals must be presented.

c. Cover notes will not be accepted.

d. An insurance policy is acceptable in lieu of an insurance certificate or a declaration under an open cover.

e. The date of the insurance document must be no later than the date of shipment, unless it appears from the insurance document that the cover is effective from a date not later than the date of shipment.

f. i. The insurance document must indicate the amount of insurance coverage and be in the same currency as the credit.

   ii. A requirement in the credit for insurance coverage to be for a percentage of the value of the goods, of the invoice value or similar is deemed to be the minimum amount of coverage required.

   If there is no indication in the credit of the insurance coverage required, the amount of insurance coverage must be at least 110% of the CIF or CIP value of the goods.

   When the CIF or CIP value cannot be determined from the documents, the amount of insurance coverage must be calculated on the basis of the amount for which honour or negotiation is requested or the gross value of the goods as shown on the invoice, whichever is greater.

   iii. The insurance document must indicate that risks are covered at least between the place of taking in charge or shipment and the place of discharge or final destination as stated in the credit.

g. A credit should state the type of insurance required and, if any, the additional risks to be covered. An insurance document will be accepted without regard to any risks that are not covered if the credit uses imprecise terms such as "usual risks" or "customary risks".

h. When a credit requires insurance against "all risks" and an insurance document is presented containing any "all risks" notation or clause, whether or not bearing the heading "all risks", the insurance document will be accepted without regard to any risks stated to be excluded.

i. An insurance document may contain reference to any exclusion clause.

j. An insurance document may indicate that the cover is subject to a franchise or excess (deductible).

Changes from UCP 500

- Provisions contained in UCP 500 articles 34, 35 and 36 have been combined into one article;
- Deletion of reference to "on their face", as this is now referred to solely in sub-article 14 (a) as a general principle covering all stipulated documents;
- Deletion of reference to pre-signed documents;
- Signing parties includes "proxy";
- Signature by an agent or proxy must indicate whether it is for or on behalf of the insurance company or underwriter;
- Cover notes issued by any party are not allowed;
- Replacement of "the date of loading on board or dispatch or taking in charge of the goods" by "the date of shipment" to reflect the new structure in the transport articles to denote the definition of shipment;
- Emphasis that the insurance must indicate the amount of insurance coverage;
- Principles of paragraphs 188, 191 and 193 of ISBP, ICC Publication No. 645, have been incorporated in UCP 600;
- Addition of the acceptability of exclusion clauses on insurance documents.

Commentary

The provisions in UCP 500 articles 34, 35 and 36 have been combined into this article. In addition, some of the concepts and principles in ISBP with regard to insurance documents have also been incorporated.

Sub-article (a) outlines the types of insurance documents that are covered, e.g., an insurance policy, insurance certificate or declaration under an open cover. An insurance document may now be signed by a proxy for or on behalf of an insurance company or underwriter. Similar language has been used to that in the transport articles (articles 19–25) to describe how an agent or proxy is to declare the capacity in which it is signing – if an insurance document is signed by an agent or proxy, it must indicate whether it has signed for or on behalf of the insurance company or underwriter.

Any party, other than an insurance company or underwriter (who signs in his own capacity), including a broker, may sign the insurance document, provided it signs as agent or proxy for or on behalf of the insurance company or underwriter.

It is a practice in the insurance industry that an insurance certificate or a declaration under an open cover may be pre-signed by insurance companies or underwriters or their agents or proxies. Such documents generally require a countersignature of the assured or other named party. Where this is the case, it must be countersigned accordingly to be acceptable under a documentary credit.

It is common for an insurance document to indicate whether it has been issued in more than one original. Sub-article (b) requires that in this event, all of the originals must be presented even if the documentary credit makes reference to a single original. An insurance document stated to be issued "in duplicate" does not necessarily infer that two originals have been created. In this event, the document marked "duplicate" will be considered to be a copy and need not be presented unless the insurance document itself includes reference to the fact that either the "original" or "duplicate" may be presented in the event of a claim. In such an event, the insurance documents marked "original" and "duplicate" must be presented.

Sub-article (c) expands the principle in article 34 of UCP 500 to state that a cover note issued by any party (not just a broker) is not acceptable.

Presentation of an insurance policy is acceptable when the credit requires an insurance certificate or a declaration under an open cover. The UCP 500 position is unchanged in the wording of sub-article (d).

However, presentation of an insurance certificate or a declaration under an open cover is not acceptable if the credit requires an insurance policy. It is understood that whilst an insurance certificate or declaration under an open cover provides proof of insurance, in the case of a claim, if there is any discrepancy of insurance coverage between the policy and the certificate or declaration under the open cover, the insurance coverage in the policy will prevail.

Some ICC national committees suggested that the date of an insurance document which is later than the date of shipment should be acceptable, since the Institute Cargo Clauses cover the "Transit Clause" as indicated in the policy. The insurance attaches from the time the goods leave the warehouse or place of storage at the place named therein for the commencement of the transit. However, the principle of examining a presentation to determine, on the basis of the documents alone, whether or not the documents appear on their face to constitute a complying presentation, applies. In respect of sub-article (e), a document examiner is not expected to check details of the specific Institute Cargo Clauses to ascertain the effective date of cover.

If the insurance document shows that the cover is effective from a date not later than the date of shipment, as determined by the appropriate transport article (articles 19–25), it is acceptable even if the date of the insurance document is later than the date of shipment. An insurance document that is dated later than the date of shipment or evidences cover effective from a date later than the date of shipment is not acceptable.

Sub-article (f) requires that the insurance document indicate the amount of insurance coverage. The amount of insurance coverage must be in the same currency as in the credit. It must be at least 110% of the CIF value or CIP value, if there is no indication in the documentary credit of the amount of insurance coverage. If the CIF or CIP value is not determinable from the presentation, the amount of insurance coverage must be calculated on whichever is greater of:

- the amount for which honour or negotiation is requested; or
- the gross value of the goods as shown in the invoice.

When a credit requires, for example, an insurance coverage for a percentage of the invoice value, that percentage amount is deemed to be a requirement for a minimum percentage of the invoice value. An insurance document presented showing the amount of insurance coverage exceeding this minimum requirement is acceptable. There is no limit on the maximum.

Sub-article (f) requires that the insurance document cover at least the risks between the place of taking in charge or shipment and the place of discharge or final destination as stated in the documentary credit. For example, if a documentary credit requiring an insurance document calls for dispatch to be effected from London Heathrow Airport to Singapore Changi Airport, an insurance document presented showing that the insurance coverage commenced from Liverpool, through to London Heathrow Airport, and until the goods arrived at Singapore Changi Airport, will be acceptable.

Sub-article (g) requires that a documentary credit specify the type of insurance coverage required, and the additional risks to be covered, if any, when an insurance document is to be presented.

The main clauses in use are:

- Institute Cargo Clauses "A", which provide cover on comprehensive basis "All Risks";
- Institute Cargo Clauses "B", which provide cover only against specified risks;
- Institute Cargo Clauses "C", which provide cover for fewer specified risks;
- Institute Cargo Clauses (Air) (excluding sending by post), which provide cover for shipment by air on "All Risks".

It is important to note that only Institute Cargo Clauses (Air) will provide cover for air shipment. It is not correct to call for an insurance document covering Institute Cargo Clauses "A" if shipment is to be effected by air.

There are other clauses specially designed to cover certain commodities (for example, frozen food, timber, coal, sugar, etc.), and these should be clearly called for in the documentary credit. Any imprecise terms, such as "usual risks" or "customary risks" must not be used. If they are used in a documentary credit, a bank will accept an insurance document as presented without regard to any risks that are not covered.

A documentary credit should not call for an insurance coverage against "all risks", as there are various types of "all risks" coverage in different markets. Sub-article (h) implies that the documentary credit should be more specific in its requirement for insurance coverage. If a documentary credit calls for insurance against "all risks", an insurance document containing any "all risks" notation or clause will be accepted without regard to any risks stated to be excluded, even if it does not bear the heading "all risks" in the document.

An insurance document containing reference to any exclusion clause is acceptable. This rule, appearing in sub-article (i), was included due to the numerous exclusion clauses currently appearing on insurance documents. These relate mainly to acts of terrorism. The insurance industry, when approached by the Drafting Group, indicated that such clauses were considered to be industry standard exclusions. During the drafting process, the Drafting Group created a list of the clauses that were being seen at that time with a view to incorporating them in this article. However, because this list could change (deletions or additions) and because of the inability to amend the list once the UCP 600 was published other than via ICC opinions approved by the Banking Commission, a decision was made to cater for any possible exclusion clauses.

The position in sub-article (j), that an insurance document indicating that the cover is subject to a franchise or excess (deductible) is acceptable, remains unchanged from that appearing in UCP 500 sub-article 35 (c).

For guidance: Franchise means an amount below which claims will not be honoured – claims above that amount are paid in full. Excess means an amount which will be deducted from the value of any claim.

Cross-references within UCP 600

- Article 2 – definition of "Credit";
- Article 3 – interpretation of "Signature";
- Sub-article 14 (d) – Standard for Examination of Documents – on data not being in conflict;
- Sub-article 14 (e) – Standard for Examination of Documents – on goods description on documents other than the commercial invoice;
- Article 17 – Original Documents and Copies;
- Article 34 – Disclaimer on Effectiveness of Documents;
- Sub-article 38 (g) – Transferable Credits – on possible increase in insurance coverage.

ARTICLE 29

Extension of Expiry Date or Last Day for Presentation

a. If the expiry date of a credit or the last day for presentation falls on a day when the bank to which presentation is to be made is closed for reasons other than those referred to in article 36, the expiry date or the last day for presentation, as the case may be, will be extended to the first following banking day.

b. If presentation is made on the first following banking day, a nominated bank must provide the issuing bank or confirming bank with a statement on its covering schedule that the presentation was made within the time limits extended in accordance with sub-article 29 (a).

c. The latest date for shipment will not be extended as a result of sub-article 29 (a).

CHANGES FROM UCP 500

- Change from reference to "the bank to which presentation is made" to "a nominated bank", and to whom such notification of receipt is to be made, i.e., the issuing or confirming bank;
- Reference to banking day as opposed to business day;
- Removal of reference to "Uniform Customs and Practice for Documentary Credits, 1993 Revision, ICC Publication No. 500" with sole reference to the above sub-article number;
- Change from "must provide a statement" to "with a statement on its covering schedule";
- Removal of the second sentence of UCP 500 sub-article 44 (b) in relation to sub-article (c);
- Refined wording in respect of the first sentence of UCP 500 sub-article 44 (b) in sub-article (c).

Commentary

The structure of sub-article (b) follows that of UCP 500 sub-article 44 (a) but relies upon the usage and definitions of "Presentation" and "Banking day". This sub-article now indicates which bank (nominated bank) is to advise which bank (issuing or confirming bank) of a presentation that has been made according to the allowance in sub-article (a). The inclusion of a rule that a nominated bank is to provide a statement to this effect on its covering schedule clearly indicates the manner in which such advice is to be conveyed – a situation that was left open by the language used in UCP 500.

In most cases, banks will probably express compliance with this condition by a statement in their schedule indicating "all terms and conditions complied with" or similar. When a nominated bank fails to provide any form of statement and this is questioned by an issuing bank or confirming bank, a subsequent confirmation of compliance with this rule will suffice for the purpose of ascertaining if a complying presentation was made.

The Drafting Group saw no reason to include the second sentence of UCP 500 sub-article 44 (b) – "If no such latest date for shipment is stipulated in the Credit or amendments thereto, banks will not accept transport documents indicating a date of shipment later than the expiry date stipulated in the Credit or amendments thereto" – due to the content of sub-articles 6 (d) (i) and 6 (e). The reference in the first sentence of UCP 500 sub-article 44 (b) to the extension of the expiry date or last day for presentation was seen to be repeating the content of sub-article (a) and therefore superfluous.

Cross-references within UCP 600

- Article 2 – definitions of "Banking day", "Confirming bank", "Issuing bank", "Nominated bank" and "Presentation";
- Sub-article 6 (d) (i) with regard to expiry date for presentation;
- Sub-article 6 (e) indicating that a presentation by or on behalf of the beneficiary must be made on or before the expiry date;
- Sub-article 14 (c) on default presentation period;
- Article 36 on Force Majeure.

Article 30

Tolerance in Credit Amount, Quantity and Unit Prices

a. The words "about" or "approximately" used in connection with the amount of the credit or the quantity or the unit price stated in the credit are to be construed as allowing a tolerance not to exceed 10% more or 10% less than the amount, the quantity or the unit price to which they refer.

b. A tolerance not to exceed 5% more or 5% less than the quantity of the goods is allowed, provided the credit does not state the quantity in terms of a stipulated number of packing units or individual items and the total amount of the drawings does not exceed the amount of the credit.

c. Even when partial shipments are not allowed, a tolerance not to exceed 5% less than the amount of the credit is allowed, provided that the quantity of the goods, if stated in the credit, is shipped in full and a unit price, if stated in the credit, is not reduced or that sub-article 30 (b) is not applicable. This tolerance does not apply when the credit stipulates a specific tolerance or uses the expressions referred to in sub-article 30 (a).

Changes from UCP 500

- Removal of reference to "circa" and "or similar expressions";
- Use of the word "tolerance" instead of "difference" to align with the heading of the article and the use of the term in sub-articles (b) and (c);
- Removal in sub-article (b) of "Unless a Credit stipulates that the quantity of the goods specified must not be exceeded or reduced" to reflect the provision in article 1 that the rules apply "unless expressly modified or excluded by the credit";
- Sub-article (c) draws no distinction between documentary credits that allow or prohibit partial shipments;
- Removal in sub-article (c) of "Unless a Credit which prohibits partial shipments stipulates otherwise" to reflect the provision in article 1 that the rules apply "unless expressly modified or excluded by the credit".

Commentary

With the increased use of the SWIFT MT7 series messages to issue and advise documentary credits, the use of terminology such as "about", "approximately", "circa" or similar expressions has diminished significantly. When a tolerance is to be applied to a credit amount, unit price or quantity, the SWIFT messages require the insertion of the actual percentage amount rather than the words "about" or "approximately". Considering that there are credits still issued in letter or telex form, the Drafting Group decided that retaining a reference to "about" and "approximate" was necessary, with the qualification that these terms equate to a tolerance of plus or minus 10%. Due to the limited, if any, use of the term "circa" or other "similar expressions", references to these terms have been removed.

The wording of sub-article (b) has been re-worded to reflect the allowance as a rule under UCP 600. There is no substantive change from UCP 500.

It is recognized that the rule in sub-article (c) has more applicability when the credit prohibits partial shipment and the emphasis is placed on "Even when partial shipments are not allowed". When a credit permits partial shipment, there is no control over how many shipments a beneficiary may make, and therefore the tolerance referred to in this rule may have minimal effect.

Cross-references within UCP 600

- Article 2 – definition of "Credit".

Article 31

Partial Drawings or Shipments

a. Partial drawings or shipments are allowed.

b. A presentation consisting of more than one set of transport documents evidencing shipment commencing on the same means of conveyance and for the same journey, provided they indicate the same destination, will not be regarded as covering a partial shipment, even if they indicate different dates of shipment or different ports of loading, places of taking in charge or dispatch. If the presentation consists of more than one set of transport documents, the latest date of shipment as evidenced on any of the sets of transport documents will be regarded as the date of shipment.

A presentation consisting of one or more sets of transport documents evidencing shipment on more than one means of conveyance within the same mode of transport will be regarded as covering a partial shipment, even if the means of conveyance leave on the same day for the same destination.

c. A presentation consisting of more than one courier receipt, post receipt or certificate of posting will not be regarded as a partial shipment if the courier receipts, post receipts or certificates of posting appear to have been stamped or signed by the same courier or postal service at the same place and date and for the same destination.

Changes from UCP 500

- Removal of "unless the Credit stipulates otherwise" to reflect the provision in article 1 that the rules apply "unless expressly modified or excluded by the credit";
- Removal of reference to "on their face";
- Determination of the date of shipment when more than one set of transport documents is presented;
- Determination of partial shipment when more than one means of conveyance within the same mode of transport is used;
- Use of reference to "A presentation consisting of ... " to be in line with the structure of sub-article 31 (b) and the definition of "Presentation" in article 2;
- Removal of reference to "dispatch notes";
- Removal of "or otherwise authenticated" due to the interpretation of signing a document in article 3;

- Inclusion of reference to "for the same destination" to bring this in line with wording in sub-article 31 (b);
- Re-ordering of the transport documents in sub-article (c) to reflect courier as the most common usage.

Commentary

Sub-article (a) creates the rule that partial drawings or shipments are allowed even when the credit is silent on this point.

The first paragraph in sub-article (b) reflects the position expressed in UCP 500 sub-article 40 (b), but explains in more detail that it applies in situations when more than one set of transport documents have been presented. The last sentence of this paragraph provides a definition of the date of shipment when more than one set of transport documents is included within a presentation bearing different dates of shipment for the same journey.

The second paragraph of sub-article (b) is new and addresses a problem that numerous banks have failed to recognize or understand under a UCP 500 credit that prohibited partial shipment. The fact that one or more transport documents have been presented does not necessarily indicate that a partial shipment has been effected. But when that or those transport documents indicate that the goods under the respective credit have been shipped or dispatched on more than one means of conveyance, within the same or different modes of transport, then a partial shipment has occurred. For example, under a documentary credit prohibiting transhipment, one or more transport documents evidencing dispatch on two or more trucks leaving on the same day, for the same destination, would be considered a partial shipment.

Sub-article (c) follows the principles expressed in UCP 500 sub-article 40 (c).

Cross-references within UCP 600

- Article 2 – definition of "Presentation";
- Article 25 on Courier Receipt, Post Receipt or Certificate of Posting.

Article 32

Instalment Drawings or Shipments

If a drawing or shipment by instalments within given periods is stipulated in the credit and any instalment is not drawn or shipped within the period allowed for that instalment, the credit ceases to be available for that and any subsequent instalment.

Changes from UCP 500

- Removal of "unless otherwise stipulated in the Credit" to reflect the provision in article 1 that the rules apply "unless expressly modified or excluded by the credit".

Commentary

There is no change to the structure and intent of this article. Although not widely used in documentary credits, the inclusion of a rule covering the consequences when a drawing or shipment schedule is not adhered to was seen to be necessary by the Drafting Group. A few ICC national committees questioned whether it was right that the failure to adhere to the schedule would result in the credit ceasing to be available for that and any subsequent drawing or shipment (unless otherwise authorized by the applicant and agreed to by the issuing bank). The view of the Drafting Group and the majority of ICC national committees, however, was that by including a specific schedule in the credit there is a definite requirement for either a drawing to be made or goods to be shipped within a specific period. Failure on the part of the beneficiary to do so could result in a financial or other risk to the applicant. Therefore, there was a need for a penalty if the beneficiary does not comply with the instalment schedule.

Cross-references within UCP 600

- Article 2 – definition of "Credit".

Article 33

Hours of Presentation

A bank has no obligation to accept a presentation outside of its banking hours.

Changes from UCP 500

None.

Commentary

The concept that a bank has no obligation to accept a presentation outside of its "banking hours" has been maintained. This rule allows a nominated bank or issuing bank to decide whether or not it will accept a presentation made by a presenter outside of its banking hours.

The reference to "banking hours" means those hours applicable locally to the nominated bank or to the issuing bank, depending on which bank the presentation is to be made to.

Cross-references within UCP 600

- Article 2 – definitions of "Presentation" and "Presenter".

ARTICLE 34

Disclaimer on Effectiveness of Documents

A bank assumes no liability or responsibility for the form, sufficiency, accuracy, genuineness, falsification or legal effect of any document, or for the general or particular conditions stipulated in a document or superimposed thereon; nor does it assume any liability or responsibility for the description, quantity, weight, quality, condition, packing, delivery, value or existence of the goods, services or other performance represented by any document, or for the good faith or acts or omissions, solvency, performance or standing of the consignor, the carrier, the forwarder, the consignee or the insurer of the goods or any other person.

CHANGES FROM UCP 500

- Change to reflect that a documentary credit may cover, not only the payment for "goods", but also for "services";
- Change to respect the specificity of the standby letter of credit by covering, not only goods or services, but also "performance".

COMMENTARY

Article 34 is the equivalent of UCP 500 article 15 except for the inclusion of "services or other performance". This is to be consistent with the statement "goods, services or performance" throughout UCP 600 – in particular in article 5. In doing so, it reflects the specific nature of a standby letter of credit covering performance.

The content of this article supports and adds further clarity to the positions taken in sub-articles 14 (a) and (d), which state respectively "A nominated bank acting on its nomination, a confirming bank, if any, and the issuing bank must examine a presentation to determine, **on the basis of the documents alone**, whether or not the documents **appear on their face** to constitute a complying presentation", and "Data in a document, when read in context with the credit, the document itself and international standard banking practice, need not be identical to, but must not conflict with, data in that document, any other stipulated document or the credit" [emphasis added].

A document checker is responsible for the examination of data appearing in a stipulated document presented under a documentary credit to the extent stated in sub-article 14 (d) and on the basis of that document alone. In so doing, the document checker must always bear in mind that such examination is restricted to the data contained in the document and not to the validity of the underlying source, content, statements or the acts of any party issuing such document, etc.

Cross-references within UCP 600

- Reference to "goods, services or performance" in article 5;
- Sub-articles 14 (a) and (d) – "on the basis of the documents alone", "appear on their face" and requirements for the establishment of non-conflicting data.

ARTICLE 35

Disclaimer on Transmission and Translation

A bank assumes no liability or responsibility for the consequences arising out of delay, loss in transit, mutilation or other errors arising in the transmission of any messages or delivery of letters or documents, when such messages, letters or documents are transmitted or sent according to the requirements stated in the credit, or when the bank may have taken the initiative in the choice of the delivery service in the absence of such instructions in the credit.

If a nominated bank determines that a presentation is complying and forwards the documents to the issuing bank or confirming bank, whether or not the nominated bank has honoured or negotiated, an issuing bank or confirming bank must honour or negotiate, or reimburse that nominated bank, even when the documents have been lost in transit between the nominated bank and the issuing bank or confirming bank, or between the confirming bank and the issuing bank.

A bank assumes no liability or responsibility for errors in translation or interpretation of technical terms and may transmit credit terms without translating them.

CHANGES FROM UCP 500

- Title includes the term "translation" to reflect the content of article 35;
- A totally new paragraph contains a provision covering documents lost in transit;
- In the disclaimer on translation, the phrase "reserve the right to transmit" has been replaced by "may transmit".

COMMENTARY

When messages, letters or documents are transmitted or sent according to the requirements stated in the documentary credit, or when a bank may have taken the initiative in the choice of delivery service in the absence of such instructions in the documentary credit, it is not liable or responsible once such messages, letters or documents leave its system or control.

However, if a bank makes a business decision to use a delivery service or method different from that specified in the documentary credit (for example, if the bank uses Courier Company A instead of Courier Company B, as called for in the documentary credit, or elects to send the documents in one courier mailing rather than two, as required by the documentary credit), the bank will be liable for any consequences arising out of any delay, loss in transit, mutilation or other errors that may arise and will not be afforded the protection of this rule.

The second paragraph clarifies the issue of documents lost in transit by creating a limited exception to the first paragraph. Specifically, it provides that if a nominated bank receives a presentation of documents and determines that it is complying, then forwards the documents to the issuing bank or confirming bank (whether or not the nominated bank has honoured or negotiated), the issuing or confirming bank must honour or negotiate, or reimburse that nominated bank, even when the documents have been lost in transit between:

- the nominated bank and the issuing bank or confirming bank, or
- the confirming bank and the issuing bank.

As a consequence, discrepant documents or documents that have not been examined and forwarded to an issuing bank or confirming bank, and are lost in transit, are not covered by article 35.

During the revision process, some national committees implied that under a documentary credit where the reimbursement condition stated "We [issuing bank] will reimburse the nominated bank upon our receipt of the documents in compliance with the terms and conditions of the credit", an issuing bank had no obligation to honour or negotiate if it did not receive the documents, i.e., if the documents were lost in transit between the nominated bank and the issuing bank. Clearly this is not desirable in documentary credit transactions.

An issuing bank that nominates a bank to act under its documentary credit is requesting that nominated bank to act towards the beneficiary to facilitate any honour or negotiation that may be requested or required by the beneficiary. Similarly, a beneficiary that makes a complying presentation but does not require the nominated bank to honour or negotiate should be protected. For an issuing bank to be able to walk away from its undertaking by virtue of documents being lost in transit would probably result in no (or very few) nominated banks' agreeing to act under their nomination until they were certain the documents had arrived with an issuing bank. A bank requested to confirm under such circumstances would surely reject such a request.

All of this needs to be put into perspective with the number of sets of documents that are sent daily between banks on a global basis against those that are lost in transit. In comparative terms, this involves minute percentages. The rule in this article merely outlines the effect of documents that are lost in transit. This position has been based to some extent on the content of ICC Opinion R.548.

ICC OPINION R.548 states

"We would very much appreciate receiving a clarification from the ICC Banking Commission.

1) A bank incorporated in Country C (the 'issuing bank') has issued an irrevocable documentary credit (the 'L/C'), available by negotiation, in favour of a company in Country S (the 'beneficiary'), payable 180 days after bill of lading date and governed by the UCP 500 rules;

2) The L/C is advised to the beneficiary through a bank in Country S (the 'negotiating bank'). The confirmation of the L/C is not requested (nor possible: no 'may add' language);

3) The L/C provides under field 78 (Instruction to pay) that the issuing bank undertakes to pay the beneficiary upon receipt at its counters of conforming documents: 'Upon receipt of full set of documents in conformity with the L/C terms, we will effect payment as per your instruction.';

4) The bank in Country S is ready to negotiate the L/C (to give value to the documents presented thereunder);

5) This being so, we understand that the risk of loss of the documents passes to the issuing bank when the L/C is realized, i.e., in our case when the bank in Country S has properly negotiated the L/C (Meetings of the ICC Commission on April 23, 1985 and May 28, 1986, R.146).

Our question is whether the type of provision mentioned under point 3) above may modify such reasoning: Does the risk of loss of documents pass to the issuing bank only upon receipt of same by it?

Analysis

The concept of this enquiry has been addressed in unpublished query TA.388 (educational response – Banking Commission meeting of May 2000) which reads: 'We issued a letter of credit and a Country I bank negotiated it. After the negotiation, the negotiating bank claimed reimbursement and received the funds from the reimbursing bank. However, we still await the documents. A thorough investigation revealed that the documents were lost in transit. We requested the negotiating bank to refund the funds, but they refused on the grounds of Article 16 of UCP 500.

It is our understanding that the negotiating bank is unable to refuse to return the funds on the basis of Article 16. They can only utilize that Article to the beneficiary or applicant. We also believe that we have no liability for the consequences arising out of loss of documents in transit.

Article 16 states: 'Banks assume no liability or responsibility for the consequences arising out of delay and/or loss in transit of any message(s), letter(s) or document(s), or for delay, mutilation or other error(s) arising in the teletransmission of any telecommunication. Banks assume no liability or responsibility for errors in translation and/or interpretation of technical terms, and reserve the right to transmit Credit terms without translating them.'

Conclusion

On the basis that the letter of credit stipulated a nominated bank to negotiate (and that bank duly acted) or that the credit was freely negotiable, a negotiating bank would be entitled to receive payment from the issuing bank. A negotiating bank is protected by the content of Article 16 in the event that documents are lost in transit.

In order that the issuing bank may carry out a review of the documents to establish compliance to the terms and conditions of the credit, it may request that the negotiating bank obtain copies of the transmitted documents.'

Conclusion

Notwithstanding the fact that the reimbursement instruction in the credit reads 'Upon receipt of full set of documents in conformity with the L/C terms, we will effect payment as per your instruction,' by virtue of Article 16 the issuing bank would be obliged to honour a compliant presentation that had been negotiated by a nominated bank but lost in transit.

The reimbursement obligation under a credit, as outlined above, is not subject to the receiving of documents by the issuing bank, but only to a compliant presentation being made to the nominated bank. The reimbursement clause in the credit does not make the reimbursement subject to the receiving of documents."

Whilst this Opinion was issued under UCP 500, it has equal application under UCP 600, in particular in relation to the fact that an issuing bank may request a nominated bank to provide copies of the underlying documents in order to establish that a complying presentation was made to that nominated bank. It must be stated, however, that there is no obligation for a nominated bank to retain copies of documents that have been presented to it.

The third paragraph of article 35 provides that an issuing bank or nominated bank is not liable or responsible for errors in translation or interpretation of technical terms in the documentary credit, and may transmit the documentary credit terms without translating them. The word "may" is to be understood in the sense that a bank is under no obligation to translate or interpret the wording of a documentary credit. This does not mean that an issuing bank should issue a documentary credit if the bank does not understand its terms and conditions.

When an advising or second advising bank receives a documentary credit in a language different from its native tongue, it may elect (as a service to its client) to translate the credit terms before advising the documentary credit and its translation to the beneficiary without any liability or undertaking. However, the advising or second advising bank may elect to send the documentary credit in the manner it was received. It should be remembered that even when a bank provides a translation, the language as well as the wording of the documentary credit remains that of the original credit.

Cross-references within UCP 600

- Article 2 – definitions of "Credit", "Complying presentation", "Issuing bank", "Confirming bank", "Negotiation", "Nominated bank" and "Honour".

Article 36

Force Majeure

A bank assumes no liability or responsibility for the consequences arising out of the interruption of its business by Acts of God, riots, civil commotions, insurrections, wars, acts of terrorism, or by any strikes or lockouts or any other causes beyond its control.

A bank will not, upon resumption of its business, honour or negotiate under a credit that expired during such interruption of its business.

Changes from UCP 500

- In the first paragraph, a new force majeure event, "acts of terrorism", has been added.

Commentary

The first paragraph makes it clear that no bank is liable or responsible for any consequences arising out of the interruption of its business due to an event that can be classified as force majeure. A number of examples of these events are cited.

The addition of "acts of terrorism" to this article is the result of a demand from a number of ICC national committees, recognizing that since UCP 500 such acts unfortunately have to be considered as a possible cause of interruption of a bank's business.

The second paragraph relates to the effect on a presenter when a credit expires during the interruption of an issuing or nominated bank's business due to a force majeure event. Such banks will not honour or negotiate upon the resumption of their business, under a documentary credit that expired during the period of interruption. If the documentary credit is restricted to a specific nominated bank, the beneficiary could present directly to the issuing bank if time permits prior to the expiry date or last day for presentation.

During the revision process, the Drafting Group discussed whether to align this article with ISP98 rule 3.14. That rule reads:

"3.14 Closure on a Business Day and Authorization of another Reasonable Place for Presentation

a. If on the last business day for presentation the place for presentation stated in a standby is for any reason closed and presentation is not timely made because of the closure, then the last day for presentation is automatically extended to the day occurring thirty calendar days after the place for presentation re-opens for business, unless the standby otherwise provides.

b. Upon or in anticipation of closure of the place of presentation, an issuer may authorize another reasonable place for presentation in the standby or in a communication received by the beneficiary. If it does so, then

    i. presentation must be made at that reasonable place; and

    ii. if the communication is received fewer than thirty calendar days before the last day for presentation and for that reason presentation is not timely made, the last day for presentation is automatically extended to the day occurring thirty calendar days after the last day for presentation."

In one of the drafts submitted to ICC national committees, article 36 included a form of "grace period" during which the beneficiary could make a presentation following resumption of the bank's business. Whilst 30 calendar days, as stated in ISP98, was considered to be too excessive for a documentary credit, a period of five banking days was offered as an alternative to the rigid structure that prevailed under UCP 500 article 17. However, the responses from ICC national committees indicated a preference for the existing structure, as banks did not seem to like the idea of an obligation without a determinable expiry date.

Cross-references within UCP 600

- Article 2 – definitions of "Credit", "Honour" and "Negotiation".

Article 37

Disclaimer for Acts of an Instructed Party

a. A bank utilizing the services of another bank for the purpose of giving effect to the instructions of the applicant does so for the account and at the risk of the applicant.

b. An issuing bank or advising bank assumes no liability or responsibility should the instructions it transmits to another bank not be carried out, even if it has taken the initiative in the choice of that other bank.

c. A bank instructing another bank to perform services is liable for any commissions, fees, costs or expenses ("charges") incurred by that bank in connection with its instructions.

If a credit states that charges are for the account of the beneficiary and charges cannot be collected or deducted from proceeds, the issuing bank remains liable for payment of charges.

A credit or amendment should not stipulate that the advising to a beneficiary is conditional upon the receipt by the advising bank or second advising bank of its charges.

d. The applicant shall be bound by and liable to indemnify a bank against all obligations and responsibilities imposed by foreign laws and usages.

Changes from UCP 500

- In sub-article (b) the banks to which this sub-article is applicable are cited;
- In the first paragraph of sub-article (c), "commissions, fees, costs or expenses" have been defined as "charges";
- In the first two paragraphs of sub-article (c), the word "party" has been replaced by "bank" (first paragraph) and "beneficiary" (second paragraph);
- New third paragraph in sub-article (c) to reflect a rule when an issuing bank requests that fees be collected in advance of advising the credit.

Commentary

All instructions provided by the issuing bank to an advising bank, confirming bank or a nominated bank in relation to the advising, confirmation, amending and honour or negotiation under a credit are given at the risk and for the account of the applicant.

An issuing bank or advising bank is responsible for its own duties and obligations. When an issuing or advising bank elects to advise a credit and any amendment thereto through another bank (advising bank or second advising bank), it is not responsible in the event that bank does not carry out the instructions. This position prevails even when the issuing or advising bank has chosen the bank to which the credit and any amendment thereto was to be advised, for further advising to the beneficiary.

The first paragraph of sub-article (c) makes clear that the issuing or advising bank is ultimately responsible to the bank to which it transmits a credit and any amendment thereto for any of that bank's charges in connection with the credit, any amendment or any associated services rendered.

The second paragraph of sub-article (c) qualifies the rule in the first paragraph of (c) by referring to situations in which the charges are stated to be for the account of the beneficiary and are not capable of being collected, i.e., the credit expires unutilized or it is utilized through another nominated bank (when the credit is freely available). The added reference to "or deducted from proceeds" emphasizes that when a bank has an opportunity to deduct all or some of its charges from the proceeds due to a beneficiary, it is not in a position to avail itself of this rule and claim those charges from the issuing bank.

The third paragraph of sub-article (c) seeks to avoid a situation in which an issuing bank looks to evade the result achieved by the rule in the second paragraph above by inserting a requirement that the advising or second advising bank should collect its fees from the beneficiary prior to advising the credit or amendment. Such a condition can place an unnecessary burden on the advising or second advising bank.

When an applicant requests a bank to issue a documentary credit in favour of a beneficiary in another country, the documentary credit will be subject to the laws and imposition of the laws in the country of both the nominated bank and the beneficiary. As a result, the applicant implicitly accepts to indemnify the issuing bank and the nominated bank against the effects that these laws may have on its handling of the documentary credit. This indemnification generally forms part of the wording contained in the counter indemnity or reimbursement agreement that exists between an issuing bank and the applicant.

Cross-references within UCP 600

- Article 2 – definitions of "Advising bank", "Applicant", "Beneficiary", "Credit" and "Issuing bank";
- Sub-article 9 (c) – definition of "second advising bank";
- Article 10 on Amendments.

Article 38

Transferable Credits

a. A bank is under no obligation to transfer a credit except to the extent and in the manner expressly consented to by that bank.

b. For the purpose of this article:

Transferable credit means a credit that specifically states it is "transferable". A transferable credit may be made available in whole or in part to another beneficiary ("second beneficiary") at the request of the beneficiary ("first beneficiary").

Transferring bank means a nominated bank that transfers the credit or, in a credit available with any bank, a bank that is specifically authorized by the issuing bank to transfer and that transfers the credit. An issuing bank may be a transferring bank.

Transferred credit means a credit that has been made available by the transferring bank to a second beneficiary.

c. Unless otherwise agreed at the time of transfer, all charges (such as commissions, fees, costs or expenses) incurred in respect of a transfer must be paid by the first beneficiary.

d. A credit may be transferred in part to more than one second beneficiary provided partial drawings or shipments are allowed.

A transferred credit cannot be transferred at the request of a second beneficiary to any subsequent beneficiary. The first beneficiary is not considered to be a subsequent beneficiary.

e. Any request for transfer must indicate if and under what conditions amendments may be advised to the second beneficiary. The transferred credit must clearly indicate those conditions.

f. If a credit is transferred to more than one second beneficiary, rejection of an amendment by one or more second beneficiary does not invalidate the acceptance by any other second beneficiary, with respect to which the transferred credit will be amended accordingly. For any second beneficiary that rejected the amendment, the transferred credit will remain unamended.

g. The transferred credit must accurately reflect the terms and conditions of the credit, including confirmation, if any, with the exception of:

- the amount of the credit,
- any unit price stated therein,
- the expiry date,

- the period for presentation, or
- the latest shipment date or given period for shipment,

any or all of which may be reduced or curtailed.

The percentage for which insurance cover must be effected may be increased to provide the amount of cover stipulated in the credit or these articles.

The name of the first beneficiary may be substituted for that of the applicant in the credit.

If the name of the applicant is specifically required by the credit to appear in any document other than the invoice, such requirement must be reflected in the transferred credit.

h. The first beneficiary has the right to substitute its own invoice and draft, if any, for those of a second beneficiary for an amount not in excess of that stipulated in the credit, and upon such substitution the first beneficiary can draw under the credit for the difference, if any, between its invoice and the invoice of a second beneficiary.

i. If the first beneficiary is to present its own invoice and draft, if any, but fails to do so on first demand, or if the invoices presented by the first beneficiary create discrepancies that did not exist in the presentation made by the second beneficiary and the first beneficiary fails to correct them on first demand, the transferring bank has the right to present the documents as received from the second beneficiary to the issuing bank, without further responsibility to the first beneficiary.

j. The first beneficiary may, in its request for transfer, indicate that honour or negotiation is to be effected to a second beneficiary at the place to which the credit has been transferred, up to and including the expiry date of the credit. This is without prejudice to the right of the first beneficiary in accordance with sub-article 38 (h).

k. Presentation of documents by or on behalf of a second beneficiary must be made to the transferring bank.

Changes from UCP 500

- "Transferring bank" replaced with "a bank" to extend the application (of no obligation to transfer) to the issuing bank, which also may be a transferring bank (see also commentary to sub-article (b));
- Provisions formerly contained in UCP 500 sub-articles 48 (a) and (b) have been combined;
- Definition of "transferable credit" changed;
- Definition of "transferring bank" changed;

- An issuing bank may be a transferring bank;
- Definition of "transferred credit" introduced;
- Deletion of language indicating that documentary credits can only be transferred once and addition of explicit wording to that effect;
- Change indicating that the first beneficiary is to give precise instructions with regard to advising amendments to the second beneficiary, as opposed to "irrevocably instruct the transferring bank" in this respect;
- Wording indicating that if a transferable credit is confirmed, the transferred credit is also confirmed;
- Consequences of failure by the first beneficiary to correct discrepancies on first demand;
- Presentation of documents to the transferring bank.

COMMENTARY

Whether or not to transfer a transferable documentary credit is the prerogative of a bank nominated to transfer a documentary credit; this is made clear in sub-article (a). This means that a nominated bank or a bank specifically authorized by the documentary credit to transfer or the issuing bank may elect not to comply with a request of the first beneficiary to transfer the documentary credit or, if it agrees to do so, may stipulate the conditions on which it agrees to transfer.

The terms defined in sub-article (b) have not been included in article 2, since they are used only in this particular article and not elsewhere in the rules.

The definition of a transferable credit in UCP 500 sub-article 48 (a) was quite complicated and unclear. In fact, a request by the beneficiary to make a documentary credit available to another beneficiary does not make the documentary credit transferable. A distinguishing feature of a transferable credit is an indication that it is transferable. In UCP 500 sub-article 48 (b), this was stated as a condition for a documentary credit to be transferred. In providing that a transferable credit means a credit that specifically states that it is transferable, the new wording makes the concept of a transferable credit clearer and more precise.

A similar situation arose with the former definition of a transferring bank. The definition of a transferring bank in UCP 500 as a bank authorized to transfer included a bank that was authorized but refused to transfer and thus could hardly be called a transferring bank. This made it necessary in UCP 500 to add to the defined term phrases such as "If the Transferring Bank agrees to transfer the Credit" or "If the Transferring Bank consents to the transfer under these conditions". The new definition in sub-article (b) simply states that the transferring bank is a bank that transfers the documentary credit.

UCP 500 provided for the possibility of a transfer only by a nominated bank but said nothing about the transfer of a documentary credit by an issuing bank. However, in practice documentary credits providing for transfer by the issuing bank are issued quite often. Sometimes an issuing bank has to perform the functions of a transferring bank when the bank originally authorized by the documentary credit to transfer does not transfer. Both of these practical realities are now covered by the definition of transferring bank.

Payment of charges is one of the conditions that has to be agreed before a bank transfers a credit and is covered by sub-article (c). However, payment of charges by the first beneficiary as the party requesting a transfer constitutes a widely accepted practice that needed to be specifically reflected in UCP 600. This is also a protection for a transferring bank, which, in most cases, will not have a direct relationship with the second beneficiary.

Sub-article (d) deals with the transfer of a documentary credit to more than one second beneficiary.

When the beneficiary uses another supplier or suppliers for production or manufacture of goods, a documentary credit may be made available in part to each of them. However, if a documentary credit prohibits partial drawings or shipments, it cannot be made available to more than one beneficiary, because of impracticalities when more than one supplier is involved and one shipment is to be effected covering each supplier's goods. In such a case, this would violate the terms and conditions of the documentary credit itself.

Although a documentary credit constitutes a transaction separate from the underlying commercial contract, as a settlement instrument it should allow the beneficiary to control the fulfillment of the contract. For this reason, any second beneficiary is not allowed to request a transfer of the documentary credit to any other subsequent beneficiary except the first beneficiary, which, after having the documentary credit or part thereof transferred back to it, can transfer it to another second beneficiary. For example, this may be required when a second beneficiary is not able to fulfil its obligations under the contract and cannot present documents under the transferred credit.

Advising of amendments under transferred credits to second beneficiaries is an issue that needs careful handling. This is covered by sub-article (e).

In practice, and for various reasons, first beneficiaries often do not wish to have all or certain types of amendments advised immediately to a second beneficiary. To accommodate the requirements of a first beneficiary, UCP 500 sub-article 48 (d) provided the first beneficiary with a choice: to irrevocably instruct the transferring bank at the moment of transfer not to advise amendments to any second beneficiary, or to issue such instructions in respect of any particular amendment as soon as it arrives or thereafter. For the benefit of both (the first and any second beneficiary), UCP 600 allows more flexibility – to request a transferring bank to advise amendments, or only certain kinds of amendments, to second beneficiaries subject to certain conditions. For example, the first beneficiary may instruct the transferring bank to advise only amendments to the credit amount and expiry date or only amendments of the requirements for documents to be presented, etc. The wording in sub-article (e) also removes the concept of the first beneficiary providing an irrevocable instruction regarding amendments. The wording in sub-article (e) does not allow the first beneficiary to change those instructions once the transferred credit has been issued, without the agreement of the second beneficiary.

An amendment is advised in whole or in part to a second beneficiary, either at the time the amendment is made to the original documentary credit (simultaneous amendment) or when the first beneficiary elects to advise the transferring bank independently as to which amendment to advise to the second beneficiary. Variations between the amendment received and the amendment advised would be restricted to the items that may be reduced or curtailed as shown in sub-article (g) or, in the case of more than one second beneficiary, the applicability of an amendment to each second beneficiary.

The instructions of the first beneficiary concerning how to treat amendments must be indicated in a request for transfer. Banks should ensure that this is a feature of any transfer request or application form that they provide for completion by the first beneficiary. The instructions of the first beneficiary regarding amendments must be reflected in the transferred credit.

If the first beneficiary allows amendments to be advised to more than one second beneficiary, the parts of a documentary credit transferred to different second beneficiaries are treated as separate documentary credits as far as amendments are concerned. This position is emphasized in sub-article (f). If an amendment is accepted by any second beneficiary, the transferred credit will be amended accordingly. If rejected, the transferred credit will remain unamended. If more than one transfer is made, each transferred credit will stand amended or unamended according to whether the amendment was made to that transferred credit and whether the second beneficiary accepted the amendment.

Needless to say, a part of a documentary credit remaining available to the first beneficiary will also be treated as a separate documentary credit as far as amendments are concerned and will be amended in accordance with the provisions of article 10.

Generally, the terms and conditions of a transferred credit must be the same as the terms and conditions of the original documentary credit. However, due to the specific purposes for which transferable credits are applied, this very often necessitates changes to a limited number of the terms and conditions of the original documentary credit. These are listed in sub-article (g). Usually, changes to the terms and conditions are made by the transferring bank at the time of transfer. These are at the request of the first beneficiary, are contained in its request or application for transfer and are subject to agreement of the transferring bank, as indicated in sub-article (a).

Sub-article (h) deals with the procedures allowing the first beneficiary to avail itself of one of the advantages of transferable credits: namely, the possibility of keeping confidential from the applicant information concerning the real price paid by the first beneficiary for the goods and the name of the actual supplier by substituting its invoice and draft (if any) for those of a second beneficiary. By substituting its invoice and draft (if any), the first beneficiary is allowed to draw for the difference between its invoice and that of the second beneficiary.

Sub-article (i) provides a waiver of the transferring bank's responsibility vis-à-vis the first beneficiary as a consequence of a delay by the first beneficiary in providing the transferring bank with the first beneficiary's own invoice and draft (if any). Taking into account day-to-day banking practice, this provision has been expanded to cover cases in which an invoice presented by the first beneficiary as a replacement for that of the second beneficiary contains discrepancies, and these discrepancies are not corrected by the first beneficiary on first demand. This is, however, limited to discrepancies that did not exist in the documents presented by the second beneficiary.

It is important to bear in mind that an issuing bank cannot refuse documents on the basis of "discrepancies" that only arise because the first beneficiary failed to present its own invoice, for example differences in unit price, amount of the invoice and in cases where the invoice is not addressed to the applicant but to a different party, i.e., the first beneficiary.

In general, a beneficiary prefers to have a documentary credit available with its local bank rather than with a foreign bank, whether that is a nominated bank or an issuing bank. A second beneficiary under a transferable credit often has the same preference. Sub-article (j) provides for the possibility to make the transferred credit available at the place to which a documentary credit is transferred. It allows the second beneficiary to make a presentation at this place up to the expiry date of the original documentary credit. At the same time, it includes a provision stating that in such a case the rights of the first beneficiary to substitute its own invoice (and draft, if any), and to draw for the difference, are not violated.

Sub-article (k) is tightly connected with sub-article (j) and is a new provision intended to further protect the rights of the first beneficiary. It covers all possible situations related to the presentation of documents under transferable credits. The principal reason for including it was to avoid cases in which the nominated bank at the place to which a documentary credit has been transferred might send the documents to the issuing or any other bank, and by doing so deprive the first beneficiary of the possibility of substituting its invoice (and draft, if any) and drawing for the difference. When the transferred credit represents a 100% transfer of the original documentary credit and there is to be no substitution of an invoice and draft (if any), a transferring bank that has not added its confirmation to the transferred credit may indicate to the advising bank that the documents of the second beneficiary are to be sent directly to the issuing bank. This would be seen as a modification of the rule in sub-article (k).

Cross-references within UCP 600

- Article 2 – definition of "Applicant", "Beneficiary", "Confirmation", "Credit", "Honour", "Issuing bank", "Negotiation", "Nominated bank" and "Presentation";
- Article 6 on availability, expiry date and date for presentation;
- Article 9 – Advising of Credits and Amendments;
- Article 10 – Amendments;
- Sub-article 14 (c), Standard for Examination of Documents, on period for presentation and period for shipment;
- Sub-article 14 (d), Standard for Examination of Documents, on data not being in conflict;
- Sub-article 28 (f), Insurance Document and Coverage, on insurance cover;
- Article 31 – Partial Drawings or Shipments.

ARTICLE 39

Assignment of Proceeds

The fact that a credit is not stated to be transferable shall not affect the right of the beneficiary to assign any proceeds to which it may be or may become entitled under the credit, in accordance with the provisions of applicable law. This article relates only to the assignment of proceeds and not to the assignment of the right to perform under the credit.

CHANGES FROM UCP 500

None.

COMMENTARY

Assignment of proceeds by a beneficiary is a regular occurrence under a documentary credit, e.g., assigning part or all of the proceeds to another supplier in respect of the cost of some or all of the goods, or to a bank when financing and/or discounting under a documentary credit has occurred. This right exists even if the documentary credit does not specifically state that it is transferable. Nothing has changed in this article that recognizes the right of the beneficiary to assign proceeds.

Whilst this position may be covered under the applicable law, it was felt by the Drafting Group that this article should remain as a necessary component of the UCP. Although some ICC national committees were in favour of removing this article, the majority supported the decision of the Drafting Group to retain it.

CROSS-REFERENCES WITHIN UCP 600

- Article 2 – definitions of "Beneficiary" and "Credit".

ICC at a Glance

ICC is the world business organization, a representative body that speaks with authority on behalf of enterprises from all sectors in every part of the world.

The fundamental mission of ICC is to promote trade and invest-ment across frontiers and help business corporations meet the challenges and opportunities of globalization. Its conviction that trade is a powerful force for peace and prosperity dates from the organization's origins early in the last century. The small group of far-sighted business leaders who founded ICC called themselves "the merchants of peace".

Because its member companies and associations are themselves engaged in international business, ICC has unrivalled authority in making rules that govern the conduct of business across borders. Although these rules are voluntary, they are observed in countless thousands of transactions every day and have become part of the fabric of international trade.

ICC also provides essential services, foremost among them the ICC International Court of Arbitration, the world's leading arbitral institution. Another service is the World Chambers Federation, ICC's worldwide network of chambers of commerce, fostering interaction and exchange of chamber best practice.

Within a year of the creation of the United Nations, ICC was granted consultative status at the highest level with the UN and its specialized agencies.

Business leaders and experts drawn from the ICC membership establish the business stance on broad issues of trade and investment policy as well as on vital technical and sectoral subjects. These include financial services, information technologies, telecommunications, marketing ethics, the environment, transportation, competition law and intellectual property.

ICC was founded in 1919. Today it groups thousands of member companies and associations from over 130 countries. National committees work with their members to address the concerns of business in their countries and convey to their governments the business views formulated by ICC.

Some ICC Specialized Divisions

- ICC International Court of Arbitration (Paris)
- ICC International Centre for Expertise (Paris)
- ICC World Chambers Federation (Paris)
- ICC Institute of World Business Law (Paris)
- ICC Centre for Maritime Co-operation (London)
- ICC Commercial Crime Services (London)
- ICC Services (Paris):
  - Events Department

ICC's programme of conferences and seminars is the essential channel for passing on the world business organization's expertise to a wider audience.

ICC Events, a Department of ICC Services, spotlights policy issues of direct concern to business such as banking techniques and practices, e-business, IT and telecoms, piracy and counterfeiting.

ICC Events also runs training courses on international arbitration and negotiating international contracts for business-people, corporate counsel, lawyers and legal practitioners involved in international trade.

  - Publications Department

ICC Publications Department is committed to offering the best resources on business and trade for the international community.

The content of ICC publications is derived from the work of ICC commissions, institutions and individual international experts. The specialized list covers a range of topics including international banking, international trade reference and terms (Incoterms), law and arbitration, counterfeiting and fraud, model commercial contracts and environmental issues.

Publications are available in both traditional paper and electronic formats from the ICC Business Bookstore.

Source Products for Global Business

ICC's specialized list of publications covers a range of topics including international banking, international trade reference and terms (Incoterms), law and arbitration, counterfeiting and fraud, model commercial contracts and environmental issues.

ICC products are available from ICC national committees which exist in over 80 countries around the world. Contact details for a national committee in your country are available at **www.iccwbo.org**

You may also order ICC products online from the ICC Business Bookstore at **www.iccbooks.com**

ICC Services
Publications Department
38 Cours Albert 1er
75008 Paris
France
Tel. (33 1) 49 53 29 23
Fax (33 1) 49 53 29 02
e-mail pub@iccwbo.org

ICC
International Chamber of Commerce
The world business organization